Praise for Bett

Weak men are everywhere. But as you'll hear Jeff say, he wrote this book with an assumption: Men actually want to be strong. *You* want to be strong. A hero awaiting the call to action lives in each of us. This book is that call. **–JASON LAASE**, Retired L.A. Metro Police Officer

Seriously?! HOW DOES HE KNOW THIS?! Somehow Jeff takes the deep, complicated inner workings of the female psyche and plainly spells them out for his tribe. Read it and you'll see why I call him the *Wife Whisperer.* Bottom line: Your marriage *needs* this one-of-a-kind book! And though it's geared toward men, I'm the one inspired to be a better woman and wife! **–BRIDGET DEPEW**, Editor at Wordly Perspectives

Gentlemen, here's your whiteboard. Your X's and O's. All the stuff we were never taught about romantic relationships. This book will change your life! I literally couldn't put it down but read it through in one sitting. It's *that* good. Get it! **–BILL LEWIT,** Head Basketball Coach, Former National Junior College Coach of the Year, Hall of Fame Coach

Don't roll the dice in your most important relationship! Jeff spells out exactly what a woman needs most from her husband. Here at 24/7, it's our go-to guide to prepare men for marriage. Every husband and husband-to-be needs to read this transformative book. **–JAVIER LABRADOR**, CEO of 24/7 Marriage

This book is a gut punch. And I mean that in the best possible way. Jeff strikes a blow to the passive behavior that keeps us small and our marriages mediocre, but with humor and an easy-to-digest "been there, done that" delivery. If playing small is no longer an option, you've found your field manual. **–CARL THOMAS**, CEO of XXXChurch

To My Clients

I'm inspired by your courage, grit, and determination to grow and become better men. Your wives don't stand a chance.

Contents

Leaving the Shire

Nature doesn't care that you're comfortable, only that you evolve.
−HARVILLE HENDRIX

My marriage story in a nutshell:

I was really good at hiding.

I hid from tension and low approval ratings at home by working a *lot*. It was easier to stay on the hamster wheel than face my inadequacies as a husband.

With over five decades of life experience under my belt, I'm convinced most of society's ills can be traced to one thing:

Men who play small, like I once did.

Men who make excuses. Men who blame others. Men who bury their emotional pain. Men who sidestep responsibility. Men who hide behind religious platitudes. Men who demand respect. Men who are afraid to learn something new. Men who pout. Men who play the victim. Men who insist everyone *else* change. Men who would rather be right than grow and become better men.

Weak men are everywhere.

But I wrote this book with an assumption: Men actually want to be strong.

You want to be strong.

When I go to the gym, I don't do bicep curls with 3-pound dumbbells. Too easy. I'm there to grow. To get stronger. To push myself. And only big demands lead to big gains.

It's why you're holding this book.

Playing small is no longer an option. Staying on the hamster wheel is no longer an option. Tolerating a tepid marriage is no longer an option. Your masculine heart has awoken.

Your new mantra:

> "I have one goal. To grow. Evolve. Become a better man. A *great* man. For me, for my family, for the world."

So yes, I'm going to push you. It's going to get uncomfortable. I'm coming after the idols of false masculinity and counterfeit strength that have made us weak. I'm going to put big demands on you. Not to crush you, but to stretch you. To make you stronger. To awaken your inner William Wallace.

Better man. Better marriage.

Always in that order.

THEORY → PRACTICE → MASTERY

Do. Or do not. There is no try.[1] (Master Yoda)

We're not "trying" anything. This isn't a one-off.

"I'll drop a few bucks on this book and give it a shot. See if any of this crap works."

Good luck with that.

No, we're moving from Theory to Practice to Mastery.[2] *That's* what you've signed up for. A lifetime of learning. A lifetime of growing and getting better.

- **Theory** is this book. It only works if you put it to work.

- **Practice** is you taking baby steps, scraping your knees, inching forward, and — *voilá!* — putting it to work. When people say to me, "Dude, your book is powerful!" I smile and respond, "Only if you do what it says."

- **Mastery** is your lifelong commitment to grow and evolve and become your best self. It's the goal line that's always moving.

Welcome to the revolution.

Everything is about to click.

The Strong ~~Silent~~ Articulate Type

You never lose by loving. You always lose by holding back.
—BARBARA DE ANGELIS

Women bond through words.

They talk. They share. They let their hair down. They emote.

Men, not so much.

Oh sure, we talk, but it's not typically how we bond.

When's the last time you and a few buddies met in New York City for a boys' weekend of sidewalk cafés, fancy desserts, lattes, deep conversation, and a slumber party at the Four Seasons?

We bond through shared activities — playing foosball, yelling at the refs during the NBA Finals, baiting hooks aboard an all-day charter.

Bro' time.

When women get together, the activity *is* talking. It's a bit oversimplified, but it's true.

Just imagine what this means for your marriage.

For your wife, words create trust. Words create intimacy. Words create emotional safety and connection. The silent, brooding male only gets the girl within the pages of erotic literature.

In the real world, he sleeps on the couch.

THE SOUND OF SILENCE

Minus her morning meditation, your wife *hates* silence.

Especially when you're around. Especially when it's obvious you're wrestling with something.

Maybe there's a problem at the office you're trying to solve. Maybe you're down on yourself over the "sudden" appearance of 20 more pounds around your waistline. Or maybe you're pissed off Tom Brady keeps winning.

Life.

But here's the thing...

Unbeknownst to you, there's another drama playing out in your home. More specifically, in your wife's head.

In the absence of words, she unconsciously fills in the missing pieces by creating a story to help her make sense of whatever it is you're contemplating or wrestling with. And since her brain, like yours, has what neuroscientists call "a negativity bias," guess what? The story she concocts in her head is *much* worse than what's playing in yours.

I'll say that again.

The story she concocts in her head is *much* worse than what's playing in yours.

That means:

- If your wife's greatest relational fear is abandonment, your silence says, "I'm making plans to leave you."

- If it's rejection, your silence says, "Leave me alone. I have lots of priorities but you're not one of them."

- If the broken record from her past insists she's not worth fighting for, your silence says, "Connecting with you is too much work. I'm only interested in you when you're meeting my needs."

Yes, all of this is happening while she chops rosemary and you sit in the next room agonizing over Tom Brady's seventh Super Bowl ring, completely oblivious to the storm that's brewing.

KILLING HER SOFTLY

I get it, life is already stressful and you're trying to spare her any additional drama, but thoughts like these are harmful to the health of your marriage:

- "I don't want to drag her into this situation at work. She has enough on her plate right now."

- "My struggle to lose weight is just that — *my* struggle, not hers."

- "Tom Brady is rich, handsome, and successful. She won't understand how I feel."

You *think* you're protecting her. What you're actually doing is throwing her to the lions. Remember, her soul feels safest when she's emotionally connected to her husband.

Feeling safe is a very big deal in the world of women. Feeling safe means she gets to soften and flower. Feeling safe means she gets to relax into your masculine energy. It means the ice melts. Frustration and anxiety ebb from her soul. Calm inhabits her body again. Feeling safe means she gets to be girly, cute, playful, fun, flirty, and provocative in the presence of her man.

All things we like.

POKE THE BEAR

Damian Duplechain, head of The Center for Marriage and Family Relationships, says this:

> Being with a silent male is scary for a woman. Especially when she notices her partner is struggling emotionally and hasn't found a way to share those feelings by putting them into words.

When you share your feelings by putting them into words, your partner won't have to create a story that can create further relationship problems. In fact, the opposite will likely occur. You'll receive physical affection and words of comfort in return.

Instead of sharing your feelings by putting them into words, imagine you decide to numb your anxiety by exploring your Facebook feed and ignoring your partner. She may experience your withdrawal as abandonment. She may even feel angry and poke the bear just to get any type of response instead of silence. All of this could create a very different outcome.[3]

INVITE HER IN

Here's an easy place to start.

It's a simple intimacy-building question, but packs more power than nuclear fusion. Use it next time you catch yourself going inward in your wife's presence:

"Would you help me process something?"

In one breath, you went from being emotionally *un*-available to emotionally available. From robot to human. From distant to present.

"Would you help me process something?"

Silence keeps her out, but your question invites her in. Silence pushes her away, but your question pulls her close. Silence says "separate," but your question says "together." Silence says, "Fend for yourself," but your question says, "We're a team."

Six words. Try it.

- "Would you help me process something? I'm wrestling with a comment my boss made today."

- "Would you help me process something? I'm really frustrated about my weight and poor eating habits."

- "Would you help me process something? I'm afraid I might hurt myself if Tom Brady wins another Super Bowl."

PUT IT TO WORK

1. Identify one thing you've been ruminating over. One thing that's bothering you. What is it?

2. Process it *with* your wife, not without her. Invite her into your headspace by putting your feelings into words. Now, don't interpret that to mean, "Talk like a woman." It can be as simple as, "Hey honey, would you help me process something? I'm frustrated with blank." *This* is how you create emotional intimacy.

Plus, the strategy or solution or encouragement you need just might be hiding inside your wife. Imagine that!

Together is better than separate.

The Thing is Never the Thing

Love change. Fear staying the same.
–MAXIME LAGACÉ

A few weeks ago, a husband who read my first book wrote to say thank you. His phone number was at the bottom of his email, so I called him. It was good timing — he was feeling a little deflated.

Him: "Jeff, all she does is criticize me. *It's constant!*"

Me: "That sucks. Give me an example."

Him: "Well, this morning in the car she told me I drive too fast. It makes her anxious."

Me: "Got it. What else?"

Him: "The other day she pointed out I need to lose 25-30 pounds."

Me: "Do you?"

Him: "Yeah, but I don't like her reminding me of it."

Me: "How long has this been going on — she complains and you defend yourself?"

Him: "Twenty years."

My next thought was, "Damn, twenty years is a long time to miss the point and perpetuate a mediocre marriage."

Been there.

NOT-SO-PEACEFUL PROTESTS

Belgian psychologist and couples coach, Esther Perel, maintains that behind every criticism from our partner is an unspoken wish or want.

Time out! That one line will transform your marriage. I'm dead serious. Read it again, only this time personalize it:

> Behind every criticism from [your wife's name] is an unspoken wish or want.

So when your wife says, *"You're playing golf AGAIN?!"* you can choose to hear it one of two ways:

1. As a critical comment

2. As a cry for connection

If you hear it as a critical comment, you'll fire back with something boneheaded like, *"Calm down! I haven't played golf in three weeks!"* Which is fine, of course, if your goal is to foster an atmosphere of chronic, low-intensity warfare in your home.

But if you quiet your ego long enough, you'll hear a much

deeper cry rising from your wife's soul. Something much more primal. True, it might feel like a jab, it might come packaged as a complaint, but those are just disguises. Lying beneath her comment is a ravenous longing.

Can you guess what for?

You.

The one she bet it all on. The one she took herself off the market for. *You.* Your time. Your attention. Your smile. Your touch. Not the scraps from your table — but *you.* The strong, present, tuned-in, badass, god-i-love-this-woman, we-need-to-do-this-more-often, irresistible version of you.

In *Hold Me Tight,* renowned psychologist Sue Johnson explains:

> What couples often don't see is most fights are really protests over emotional disconnection. Underneath the distress, partners are asking each other: "Can I count on you? Are you there for me? Will you respond when I call? Do I matter to you? Do you need me?" The anger, the criticism, the demands, are really cries to their lovers, calls to stir their hearts, to draw their mates back in emotionally and reestablish a sense of safe connection.[4]

"You're playing golf AGAIN?!" is really her way of saying:

> "I miss you. I miss *us*. I was really hoping to spend some time with you this weekend. Remember when Saturday was *our* day?"

It's not about golf.

It never is.

YOUR NEW MANTRA

Seven years ago, when I made personal evolution my highest value, I taught myself to lean *into* critical comments. It was difficult at first, but made easier when I adopted the mantra, "Growth moment. Growth moment. Growth moment."

That, and a few deep breaths, will move your nervous system out of "fight or flight," quiet your lizard brain, and allow you to address your wife's unspoken wants, which, in turn, leads to greater closeness and intimacy in your marriage.

Stay on the surface — make it about golf — and you'll completely miss the point. Bicker about "the thing" and you'll be at each other's throats for twenty *more* years.

So then, when criticism arises, your job as a husband is to lead the conversation in a radically different direction. To bring her unspoken wants to the surface and acknowledge them. To answer her heart's cry. I'll give you an example of how to do that in a moment, but first, let's finish laying our foundation. A criticism is three things:

1. An unspoken want (Her)

2. A growth moment (Me)

3. An opportunity for greater intimacy (Us)

OK, back to our imaginary scene. You're loading your clubs into the SUV when she opens the front door and shrieks, *"You're playing golf AGAIN?!"*

Your first win is to remember ... it's not about golf.

Your second win is to say *nothing* from the driveway. Instead, take a deep breath, pull your shoulders back, look your wife in the eyes, and make a beeline for her. Don't stop until you're in her physical space. I'm talking a foot or two away. Let her feel your masculine, in charge, i'm-leading-us-in-a-different-direction energy.

GET. IN. HER. SPACE.

Without even opening your mouth, you're bombarding her psyche with powerful, healing messages:

- "There's distance between us, and I'm *not* OK with it."

- "I'm not avoiding you or your pain anymore. That's the old, pansy-ass me."

- "You matter to me. Your *heart* matters to me. Whatever I've done to upset you matters to me. Our marriage is Priority Number One. Get used to it."

Oh, and while you're moving in her direction, don't say, *"Shhhhhh. The neighbors might hear you."* Screw the neighbors. You have a princess to rescue.

You're in her space. *Check*. Eyes locked on hers. *Check*. Now let's put words to work:

You: "It sounds like someone is feeling unimportant. That sucks. Because that someone is the most important someone on the planet to me. And if she's feeling overlooked — like she's not a priority anymore — then I am *seriously* off my game. Saturday used to be our day, didn't it? Damn, I've really let that slip.

"You know what we need? Some *us* time. You. Me. Without the kids. How about this afternoon? I'll ask my parents to come over early, say 3-ish. Let's you and I get outta here and go do something fun. Spend the rest of the day together [smile]. I would really like that."

Now kiss her like you mean it.

Lastly, do you notice what's missing?

No sniveling.

"I'm sorry, dear. I-I-I-I won't play golf today."

Disgusting.

She doesn't want to be your mother — she wants to be your wife. She wants you to pursue her. Romance her. Fight for her heart. She wants her man to be the man. To take the lead in building a strong and sexy marriage. Anything less is weak and unattractive.

THE REST OF THE STORY

Remember the guy we opened this chapter with? The one who drives too fast and needs to lose some weight around the middle?

A few days after we spoke — with a little guidance from me — he had a conversation with his wife that went something like this:

> **Him:** "Hey babe, you haven't been shy about pointing out that I need to lose some weight. You must feel passionately about it. Instead of getting defensive, I really want to hear you. I want to understand where you're coming from. Do me a favor and finish this sentence: 'I want you to lose 30 pounds *because*...'"

> **Her:** "I want you to lose 30 pounds because we're in our mid-50's, and extra belly fat can lead to a whole host of health issues for people our age. I hate the thought of losing you. I hate the thought of being alone. I want you to live a long time, so we can spend our golden years together. Traveling. Seeing the world. Enjoying quality time with our children and grandchildren. I want you to be healthy and fit, not stuck in a hospital bed somewhere. I want you by my side... for as long as possible. That's what I want."

You can defend yourself when your wife criticizes you. You can get upset and act like a baby because you don't like her tone or choice of words.

You can argue in circles for twenty years...

Or you can turn each critical comment into a growth moment and build a better marriage.

The thing is never the thing.

The "V" Word

Vulnerability is sexy.
−VANESSA VAN EDWARDS

Man likes sex.

Woman likes sex (with sexy man).

Woman makes it easy by telling man what's sexy to *her*.

Wife Magnet makes it even easier by reminding man of what woman said.

Woman says, "Vulnerability is sexy."

Man says, "Nah."

Man sleeps alone.

Her Half-Assed Effort Detector (And Its Origin)

Do what you did in the beginning of a relationship and there won't be an end.

–TONY ROBBINS

Every married woman has a half-assed effort detector. They can smell *passive* and *uninspired* from a mile away. It's like a superpower.

You understand why, of course.

It's because they know *exactly* what all-in looks like.

Your wife saw it up close when you courted her.

She's *seen* your best. She *knows* what you're capable of. You're the one who taught her what it feels like to be chosen. To be cherished. To be your number one.

Courtship is a man's way of saying:

- "This is what I'm promising — more of this."

- "This is what you'll be saying yes to — more of this."

- "This is what our marriage will look like — more of this."

- "This is what you have a *right* to expect — more of this."

This is where most marriages die. This is the bait and switch that so many men fail to recognize and so many women fail to recover from.

Let's read those statements again. Except this time they're questions. And this time, imagine it's your wife who's talking. The italicization of each bullet point is to emphasize her tone — a mélange of surprise, awe, restrained elation, incredulity, and pure joy. She's practically jumping out of her skin:

- *"Shut the front door! This is what you're promising?! More of this?!"*

- *"You mean, this is what I'll be saying yes to?! A lifetime of this?!"*

- *"Are you serious?! This is what our marriage will look like?! For real?!"*

- *"This is what I have a right to expect?! Every day?! Forever?!"*

Whoops.

It's the reason my own marriage collapsed. I promised so much but delivered so little.

My brothers…

We don't do half-assed at the gym. We don't do half-assed at work. We don't do half-assed with our hobbies or favorite sports teams. Yet we label our wives "over-reactive" and "impossible to please" when they refuse to eat our leftovers.

It's why there was an undercurrent of resentment running through my home. I felt it. I knew it was there. I just didn't know *why* it was there.

Like me, you thought, "I'm sick of picking up your dirty socks!" was about socks.

Not even close.

Let me translate: "You tricked me! You promised me your best! This is *not* your best!"

Not even close.

MODERN COURTSHIP AND THE FALL OF CIVILIZATION

Therein lies the crime of modern courtship.

The goal is to get the girl. It's not to learn how to love and cherish the girl.

It's to get her to say yes.

We're good at going all-in when it means getting a woman to say yes. But imagine if the goal of courtship was to learn and grow and become a better man. The kind of man the girl would *keep* saying yes to, month after month, year after year.

And imagine if the goal of courtship became the goal of marriage.

Imagine if you *continued* to evolve.

What kind of marriage would you have?!

What kind of man would you be?!

DECISION TIME

That brings us to the end of this chapter and the two radically different choices you're faced with:

1. **Do nothing** — Continue to commit fraud in your marriage and rejoin your wife on the resentment-go-round.

2. **Take action** — Commence "Courtship 2.0" and replace Idris Elba as The Sexiest Man Alive.

Message me if your wife is checked out and you'd like help courting her again (the right way). I offer private coaching to husbands determined to win their wives back.

That's *my* superpower.

Husbands Go First

*Stand true to your calling to be a man. Real women will always
be relieved and grateful when men are willing to be men.*

–ELISABETH ELLIOT

Five words that change everything:

Be first in your marriage.

- The first to smile
- The first to listen
- The first to call bullshit on yourself
- The first to say, "You know something, you're right"
- The first to forgive
- The first to write a note
- The first to put your phone away
- The first to massage her shoulders
- The first to talk about the elephant in the room

- The first to say, "I want you"

- The first to ask for help

- The first to see a marriage counselor

- The first to plan a date night

- The first to ask, "If you had one piece of marriage advice for me, what would it be?"

The cult of mediocrity has turned us into cry babies. Spoken in my best whiny, high-pitched, entitled-husband voice:

> "But why do *I* always have to go first?! Why do *I* always have to be the one to initiate everything?! *Waaaahhh!*"

That's like a cow complaining, "Why do *I* always have to provide the milk?"

You're a cow. You make milk. It's what you do. It's your contribution to the world. Quit whining and make milk. Feed us.

> Dear Husband,
>
> You're an Initiator. You initiate. You go first. *It's what you do.* It's your contribution to the family that bears your name. Quit complaining and go first. We're counting on you.
>
> P.S. Get really good at it and your stock will go through the roof!

It's how you got here, right?

You went first. You led the charge. You got her number. You asked her out. You asked her out again. You leaned in for that first kiss. You showed up and surprised her at work. Or outside her Anthropology Class. You made it official: "This is my girlfriend." You picked her up at the airport. You washed and detailed her car. You helped her move. You were relentless! You brought her home to mom and dad — *"I think she's the one."* And yes, you borrowed money, bought a ring, chose the spot, and got down on one knee. You were the first to say, "This is for keeps. *Death* is the only thing strong enough to remove me from this race."

It was your role then…

It's your role now.

Accept your role. *Relish* your role. *Lean into* your role. Especially if you've been passive — stuck in Marriage Hell — waiting for your wife to go first. It's where most of us retreat after courtship. We trade strength for weakness. Active for passive. Leading for following. By default, we force our wives into their masculine energy and they resent us for it.

Your wife would much rather *you* lead the charge. Your shoulders are broader than hers for a reason.

A TRUE STORY

I want to tell you a "go first" story from my childhood. There's a lesson in it for your marriage.

It was a warm summer day in Sea Bright, NJ. Local families were enjoying a day at the beach. My friends and I spent the morning zig-zagging back and forth between the ocean and the pool. The ocean was always colder, so we'd bodysurf until we started shivering, then head up to the pool to thaw and generally cause mayhem. One of our favorite pastimes was cannonballing the adults who sat poolside — especially fully-dressed dads on their lunch breaks — soaking them in a wall of water.

We were terrors.

At some point in the afternoon, my waterlogged friends and I would gather our pennies, leave the beach club, and walk across Ocean Avenue to buy candy and ice cream. On this particular day, we sat and enjoyed our cones on a dock near the drawbridge that connects the coastal towns to the mainland. To our surprise, a few teenage boys walking across the bridge towering above us climbed over the railing and jumped into the swift-moving river 30 feet below. We were in absolute awe. The beach club and its 4-foot high-dive would never look the same!

Without pausing to see if they survived the jump, we scrambled to the top of the bridge to upstage the older boys. Mustering all the bravado an 11-year-old could muster, I climbed over the railing and stood on the 3-inch ledge, staring terrified into the abyss below. In that moment, I learned the first lesson of bridge jumping: 30 feet looks like 60 from the top.

I talked my friend Robert Soleau into joining me on the ledge. Facing the water, with our backs against the railing and our heels holding on for dear life, we made a solemn pact: We would join hands and leap on the count of three. I shouted above the din of boat horns and passing cars, *"Readyyyy?! Onnnne … This is it! Twoooo … No turning back! THREE!"* But instead of jumping, I clasped the railing with my left hand, and threw Robert off the bridge with my right.

It takes an 80-pound boy just 1.37 seconds to fall 30 feet and disappear into the murky depths below. Waiting for his head to break the surface and reappear, however, felt like an eternity. But the moment it did, I leapt with gusto! In a nanosecond, my primitive brain ran the calculations and concluded, "A boy of similar stature jumped and didn't die. The threat of death by jumping is now lower than the threat of death by expulsion from peer group. *Jump!*"

That was 1977. My amygdala was right. I'm still alive.

Fast forward to 2019 …

I'm encouraging a client (Dave) to make a bold move in his broken marriage and he's pushing back. He said it felt "too risky."

I replied, "It *should* feel risky. It *should* feel unfamiliar. This is new territory for you. It's also your opportunity to go first. To raise your hand and say, '*I'll* be the one to assume responsibility and risk my heart getting broken.'

"When you do, two powerful things happen: First, you lay the foundation — not for the marriage you *have*, but for the marriage you *want*. That foundation looks like this:

- Dave goes first.

- Dave leads the way.

- Dave sets the example.

- Dave says, 'Follow me.'

- Dave moves from the background — where's he's been — to the foreground — where he belongs.

"Second, you carve out a path for Gigi to walk down. Remember, her day of decision is coming. Her day of ignoring the skeptic in her head is coming. Her day of leaping into the unknown is coming. She'll face the same feelings of resistance and aversion you face. Your brave example will allow *her* to be brave. Dave putting his family's greater good above his own personal good creates space for Gigi to do the same.

"Take it from me, jumping off a 60-foot cliff is *much* easier for the second person."

Going first takes guts. Going first takes spine. Going first — doing the right thing because it's the right thing — is a hero move.

It's also part of your job description.

Husbands go first.

Husbands leap first.

PUT IT TO WORK

1. There's something in your home that's begging for your leadership. Begging for you to go first. What is

it? Where have you been passive or crying, *"Unfair! I was the first to apologize last time!"*? Where have you been acting more like a bystander than a strong, present, engaged man?

2. What does leading the charge look like in your situation? Is it being the first to plan a date night? Contact a marriage counselor? Call bullshit on yourself? Forgive your wife for something?

3. What's one thing you can do *today* to build the marriage you want? To become more leader and less follower.

4. Do it now.

Success is not a big step in the future. It's a small step taken right now. (Jonatan Mørtensson)

Why You Should Touch Your Wife More

What a grand and beautiful force — the immense and wildly unappreciated power of human touch.

-ATTICUS

Here's a simple way to combat intimacy anorexia[5] and put some meat back on the bones of your most important relationship. Put it to work whether you're spending a rainy weekend together on the couch or racing past your wife on your way out the door Monday morning. Three reasons to follow the science and touch your wife more:

1. TOUCH PROMOTES TRUST & WELLBEING

Dachner Keltner, leading researcher on the science of touch at UC Berkeley, says, "Touch signals safety and trust. It turns off the threat switch. It calms cardiovascular stress. It soothes. Studies show that touching patients with Alzheimer's disease, for example, can have huge effects on helping them relax, make emotional connections with others, and reduce their symptoms of depression."[6]

2. TOUCH PROMOTES COOPERATION

Touch reinforces mutual cooperation between our primate relatives, who use touch and grooming to reduce tension and build social alliances. And while gorillas and lemurs spend *hours* each day running their fingers through each others' hair, psychologist Robert Kurzban found that a single touch offered to your wife — even a quick pat on the back — makes her much more likely to cooperate with and act favorably toward you.[7]

3. TOUCH PROMOTES BONDING

Physical touch triggers the release of oxytocin — "the love hormone" — producing feelings of well-being and helping us bond with the people we touch. It's one of the reasons we shake hands with strangers. It increases the chances they'll treat us favorably, even if we've just met.

Dachner Keltner of UC Berkeley again: "A recent study found when librarians pat the hand of a student checking out a book, the student says he or she likes the library more and is more likely to come back."[8]

A pat on the hand!

Find your list labeled "Ways to Manipulate My Wife and Get What I Want," and cross off "pout," "play the victim," "work late," and "withhold affection." In large capital letters, write "TOUCH HER MORE" instead.

And in case you're not in awe yet...

EDWARD HEALING HANDS

OK, so physical touch between couples is beneficial for a number of reasons, but now we have scientific proof *pain relief* is one of them. A recent study out of the University of Colorado Boulder shows that holding hands with your partner reduces pain.

Reduces pain!

The study stemmed from the real-life experience of neuroscientist and researcher, Pavel Goldstein. During his wife's labor and delivery of their daughter, he found that when he held her hand, her labor pains eased off. "My wife was in pain, and all I could think was, 'What can I do to help her?' I reached for her hand and it seemed to help," he recalls. "I wanted to test it out in the lab. Can one really decrease pain with touch, and if so, how?"[9]

The couples enlisted for the study had been together for at least a year. Researchers monitored their brain waves while they were put through a series of scenarios — sitting in separate rooms, sitting together but not touching, and sitting together holding hands. Each scene was repeated while mild heat pain was applied to the forearm of the female participant.

When the couples were in the same room, whether or not they were touching, their brain waves synchronized. This syncing was the strongest when the pair were holding hands and the woman was in pain. When they weren't holding hands, the brain wave syncing declined and her pain intensified.

Goldstein explained to *CU Boulder Today*: "It appears that pain totally interrupts this interpersonal synchronization between couples, and touch brings it back."[10]

The study revealed another remarkable finding: When the man was more empathetic to his partner's pain, the syncing increased and her pain subsided even further. "You may express empathy for a partner's pain, but without touch it may not be fully communicated," Goldstein said.[11]

I WANNA HOLD YOUR HAND

Today's lesson:

Sitting on the same couch isn't enough.

Having dinner at the same table isn't enough.

Sleeping in the same bed isn't enough!

She needs you to touch her.

To hold her.

You.

You have healing hands.

Miracle-working hands.

Literally!

Your touch matters.

Holding her hand, rubbing her shoulders, giving her a long hug (or a short one) *matters*.

When your wife shares her pain with you — whether it's physical or emotional — she's not making small talk! She's opening the door and inviting you in. She's inviting you to move in her direction. To go deeper as a couple. To build greater bonds of trust and intimacy.

Now is not the time to run off.

Now is not the time to check your phone.

Now is the time to be present.

To listen with empathy.

To hold her like you mean it.

So...

Touch her.

Hold her.

As early and often as possible.

Especially when she's in distress.

And when I touch you I feel happy... inside.[12]

Lennon & McCartney were onto something.

Apologize Like a Man

Never wound a snake. Kill it.

−HARRIET TUBMAN

Does your wife still gripe about something you did two years ago? 20 years ago?

I just helped a client remove the stinger from a careless move he made before he and his wife were married — 26 years ago! She was *still* suffering. *Still* agonizing over it. *Still* using it against him.

I'll tell you that story — The Sofa Chair Incident — in a moment. But first, here's something that took me 48 years to learn:

"I apologize" is not an apology.

"I'm sorry" is not an apology.

When my son huffs and puffs and says with a surly attitude, *"OK! I'm sorry!"* after getting caught doing something stupid or selfish, I want to fire back, "For *what*, exactly?!"

I don't, of course, but when he calms down, I walk him through this simple four-point outline. It's what I use when I've blown it and hurt him or someone else.

1. OWN IT

Our wives don't lose faith in us because we do something stupid or selfish. We all do! We all blow it! We're all a work in progress! No, our wives lose faith in us because we do something stupid or selfish and never *acknowledge* it. Never *own* it.

Not owning it sounds like this:

- "OK, OK, you don't need to freak out."
- "It was an accident... *geeeez*."
- "Well, you did the same thing a few days ago."
- "Why are you getting so bent out of shape?! I *said* I was sorry!"
- "Is it that time of the month?"

Owning it, on the other hand, sounds like this:

- "Crap, I screwed up."
- "That was terrible judgment on my part."
- "I was wrong to use that tone with you, period."
- "I could've called to say I was running late."
- "You're right. That was selfish of me."

Number one, grow a pair and *own* it.

2. GRIEVE IT

Your wife needs to know she's not the only one who's upset. She needs to know you regret hurting her. Use words that are strong and emotive:

- "I feel awful about what I did. "
- "You didn't deserve to be treated that way."
- "I really hurt you, didn't I?"
- "I *hate* that I let you down."
- "What was that like for you?"

This is how you help her feel heard. It's how you emotionally take her side. *Not* feeling heard — *not* feeling connected to you — is why she's distant. It's why your marriage is running on fumes. It's why you were in serious trouble long before you became aware of it.

Grieve what you did. Feel her pain. Acknowledge her pain.

3. ASK IT

If you've truly owned it and expressed remorse, it's time to ask, "Will you forgive me?"

Four words. That's it.

No promises. No guarantees. Just, "Will you forgive me?"

Let it hang there. Be OK with the silence. Be OK with the awkwardness. You won't die. She's processing ... let her process. Don't fill that awkward space with nervous, useless words. Stand tall in that awkward space. The moment might be awkward, but *you* don't have to be.

"Will you forgive me?"

The next move is hers. You've moved in her direction, it's her turn to move in your direction. To respond. To forgive you if she's ready to.

4. FIX IT

Notice, this comes *last*, not first, which is our typical MO.

OK, imagine it's a weekday morning. You're in the kitchen — in a hurry — trying to get out the door. In your haste you accidentally knock over your wife's morning smoothie.

She explodes, *"Auggghhh!* You're always in such a hurry! Can't you manage your time better?! It took me 20 minutes to make that smoothie! It has like a hundred ingredients in it!"

You haven't read this chapter yet, so you say, "Alright, alright, calm down, it's just a smoothie! I'll make you another one."

No ownership. No emotional connection. No taking her side. No forgiveness moment.

And do you know what else?

No growth. No progress.

Let's be honest, if you're in a hurry to get out the door every morning, your time management probably *does* suck. It probably *does* need improving.

But no, right to the fix we go.

Make amends — of course! Whip her up another smoothie — of course! Better yet, take her to your local juice bar and make an impromptu date out of it. But don't *start* there, *end* there!

Own it. Grieve it. Ask it. Fix it.

THE SOFA CHAIR INCIDENT

In case there's an open psychic loop in your wife's brain that needs to be closed, stemming from a dumb or careless move of yours 30 days or 30 years ago, here's that story I promised.

My client Kevin and his wife Lisa were engaged at the time, enjoying themselves at a swanky cocktail party. Lisa excused herself to use the restroom and Kevin took a seat on — you guessed it — a sofa chair.

Lisa returned and did what a lot of young, energetic, playful women do when they're feeling very connected to their future husband: She sat down — not on the armrest — but on his lap.

Fun, right?

Kevin didn't think so. He jumped out of the chair like hot coffee had just been spilled on his lap — flustered and a little miffed. The message was loud and clear: "*That* was a stupid thing to do!" Later, he said something like, "You're overreacting. I was hot and didn't want anyone sitting on my lap. That's all."

(**PSA:** Guys, when your wife sits on your lap, I don't care if you've just had a vasectomy or hip replacement surgery, smile, put your arm around her waist, and pull her close.)

Fast forward 26 years. Kevin and Lisa have been married for a quarter century and have three children together. They're currently separated, and Lisa is still bringing up The Sofa Chair Incident. And each time, without fail, Kevin protests, "We've talked about this a *gazillion* times. I've apologized over and over again. Let it *go* already!"

That's his Fix It attempt — "Just drop it, Lisa, and it will all go away."

When he shared the story I just shared with you, I said, "Kevin, it's not the event. It's the meaning Lisa gave *to* the event. It's not the actual insult or personal slight. It's the story *about* the insult or personal slight she's been telling herself for 26 years:

- "There must be something wrong with me."

- "Kevin and I will never be close."

- "He'll never care for me like other men care for their wives."

- "He's incapable of warmth."

- "Our marriage is more like an arrangement than a relationship."

- "What husband would *do* that?!"

"It's an open psychic loop that needs to be closed. Talking about it one more time the same way you've always talked about it won't help! We need a completely different approach. Change is not in the known. It's in the unknown. It's in what you *haven't* tried yet. So, what does Lisa need to hear from Kevin that she hasn't heard yet? *That's* our guiding question."

REMOVING THE STINGER

Me: "Do you have a sofa chair in your home?"

Kevin: "No, but there's one in the bay house."

Me: "Great. The next time you're there, I want you to bring Lisa to the room where the sofa chair is, point to it, and say this:

"'26 years ago you sat on my lap in a chair just like this one, and I jumped out from under you, half-spilling our drinks. That moment really hurt you. I think it's still hurting you, like an open loop that's never been closed. I would give *anything* to relive that moment. You were being playful and trying to connect with me. Like a fool, I got up because I was hot and uncomfortable. I was so concerned with how *I* felt, that I didn't consider how *you* must have felt when I stood up so abruptly. I bet you felt humiliated. Like a nuisance. Like you did something wrong. No, *I* (point to yourself) was the one who did something wrong! *I* was the one who blew it. What should have been a tender moment between us became a black mark on our marriage. That crushes me.

" 'Lisa, I am so, so, sorry. You're the last person on the planet I'd ever want to hurt. Would you forgive me for being so shallow? So foolish. So callous. So disconnected from you that night. Would you forgive me?' "

And depending on how it goes, I told him to sit down on that sofa chair and ask, "Would you do something else for me? Would you sit on my lap and let me hold you?"

And guess what?

She did.

I hope you feel the *weight* of that, the raw masculine strength of that. In the space of just a few minutes, a 26-year-old monolith of resentment and misunderstanding heaved, buckled, and fell to the ground — never to rise again.

This is how you remove the stinger. This is how you *build* trust and intimacy instead of eroding it.

Go ahead, apologize like a man.

[**Note:** This chapter is an excerpt from my Master Class.]

Little is the New Big

Little things console us because little things afflict us.

–BLAISE PASCAL

While speaking with a client this week, the subject of coffee came up. Specifically, the cup of coffee he used to brew for his wife each morning, so it was ready and waiting for her when she came downstairs.

Used to brew.

I asked why he stopped.

"I dunno. Over time, she expected it and stopped thanking me."

Quickly realizing his marriage coach was on the other end of the line, he added, "But I guess I should do it 'just because' and not look for gratitude."

Sounds miserable.

Here's what I told him. Four things:

1. Having your wife expect you to do little things for her is a plus, not a minus. In the world of women, "thoughtful" is sexy. "Considerate" is sexy. A husband who can be counted on is sexy. In the words of Mae West, "Too much of a good thing can be wonderful."

2. Every thoughtful gesture, even an "unnoticed" one, is money in your marriage account. In a moment of frustration, she's apt to think, "You know, my husband does so many little things for me that I overlook. He makes my coffee every morning even though I stopped thanking him months ago. He's a good man. *Snap out of it, girl!*"

3. True, she might not thank you every day. She might stop thanking you altogether. No matter. It's still a powerful husbands-go-first start to *your* day. It builds your leadership muscle. Your initiative muscle. Your i'm-going-to-love-and-serve-my-wife-when-it's-appreciated-and-when-it's-not muscle. It sets the tone in your family. It's the stark opposite of the relationship–destroying, "I'll give more to this marriage as soon as she does."

4. Trust that in the bigger scheme, your efforts *will* be rewarded. You may not hear, "Thank you for making my coffee this morning," but you'll enjoy a closer connection. Greater trust. Greater intimacy. Your wife will be softer toward you. More willing to overlook an offense. Don't fall prey to the tendency we all share — to overvalue the things we can measure and undervalue the things we can't.

SMALL AND MUNDANE FOR THE WIN

In his post, "Don't be Fooled, Real Romance is All About the Little Things," Tom Burns writes:

> My definition of what constitutes romance has definitely evolved over the past two decades. When I was younger, I'll admit, I was all about the grand sweeping gesture. I bought extravagant gifts. I planned secret vacations. But as I got older, I realized my grand gestures were more about making *me* feel like a hero than giving my wife what she actually wanted.
>
> She doesn't want bombast, she wants thoughtfulness. She wants me to load the dishwasher after she goes to bed. She wants me to say I'll clean out the garage and actually follow through with it. She wants to see me love and appreciate her by walking the walk and doing the work, rather than hiding behind a price tag or a clichéd gift.
>
> True romance is all about the small things. The tiny, quiet moments that scream out that you know and love someone down to their core. That's what our romance looks like now. It's small and it's mundane and it means *everything*. And it took me far too long to realize that.[13]

ONE LAST THING...

In case she does say, "Thank you for making my coffee this morning," *please* don't respond with, "You're welcome." [gag]

Domestic robots can be programmed to do that.

Answer her bid for connection (and 10X the impact of your small act of kindness) with this:

> "Do you know why I do it? Because I love you. [smile] Because I'm crazy about you. Because I know it helps you start your day strong. And that matters to me. You will *always* be my priority."

This is where you step into her space and kiss her.

Unless, of course, she's already kissing you.

> Kindness costs me so little and rewards me so well.
> (Howard Fast)

PUT IT TO WORK

1. Is there something small, thoughtful, and kind you *used* to do for your wife? What is it?

2. Restart those engines! Not to impress her. Not to get something in return. But to stretch yourself. To grow. To become a man worth following.

Embrace Your Inner Detective

His attentive treatment of her had nothing to do with the presumption she was weak, and everything to do with the conviction she was valuable.[14]

—ANGELA BLOUNT

Imagine you and your wife are driving from L.A. to Vegas for the weekend. Or from New England to North Carolina for a family reunion. An hour into the trip she asks, "Do you need to stop and use the restroom?"[15] You don't, of course, because you didn't devour a large chocolate mocha latte during the first 10 minutes of the trip, so you answer, "Nope. I'm good."

Big mistake. Here's why:

Women don't typically come out and say what they want.[16] After all, what's romantic about that? "I need to pee. Pull over." Boring. Any robot can issue an order. Instead, they give us clues and expect us to do some digging in order to *uncover* what they want. They drop a few crumbs to see if we care enough to follow the trail.

So then, her question is never really a question, but a hint. Say this out loud if it helps: "Her *clues* are my *cues*." No, not to throw your hands up in frustration, but to don your deerstalker and begin playing detective. It's about to get fun! Remember, the trail always leads to the treasure. Here's a sample Sherlock-worthy response to her question-that's-not-really-a-question:

> **Her:** "Do you need to stop and use the restroom?"
>
> **You:** "Well, we've been on the road for an hour now. How are you feeling, babe? Do *you* need to use the restroom?"
>
> **Her:** "Mmm, I don't know."
>
> **You:** "It looks like you've finished your latte. Would you like me to pull over at the next rest stop?"
>
> **Her:** "I think I'll be OK."
>
> [pause for dramatic effect]
>
> **You:** "You know, I think stopping is a good idea. I'd like to stretch my legs. Plus, we've got 30-40 miles of desert ahead of us before the next town. We should probably refuel just to be safe. And we're probably both ready for a bathroom break."
>
> **Her:** "OK, honey."

When she reaches across the console for your hand and gives it a little squeeze, it's *much more* than a little squeeze. It's her way of saying, "I feel loved. I feel cared for. I feel lucky to have you."

She's dancing on the inside.

She'd turn on some music and dance on the outside too, right there in her seat, if she didn't have to pee so bad.

The treasure — in case you were wondering — is her heart. One that trusts you. Feels safe with you. Feels connected to you. A heart that respects and adores her husband. These are the headwaters for a strong and sexy marriage.

LATIN FOR "DUMB"

Standard-issue marriage advice to women says, "Your husband's not a mind reader. Tell him what you want."

"Yeah!" shout all the men within earshot. "We're not mind readers! Just tell us what you want! Don't make it so complicated! Don't make us have to work so hard!"

Here's the problem: While it sounds reasonable to the logical hemisphere of *your* brain, it bounces off hers. When you say, "I'm not a mind reader, just tell me what you want," she hears:

"I've already won your heart. I've already cracked the code. I'm done breaking a sweat for you. The chase is over! Sorry, but you're just not that interesting anymore. Get used to me taking you for granted. Get used to a marriage that's dull and predictable."

Or, even worse:

"Can't you be more like my guy friends?! More rational. More linear. Less nuanced. Less mysterious. I just wish you'd stop acting like such a *woman*."

And you wonder why she's hardly ever in the mood.

All this time — unbeknownst to you — you've been insisting that your wife *tone down* her sex appeal. Be *less* amorous. The word "sensual" comes from the Latin "sensualis," meaning, "endowed with feeling, sensitive." Regardless of her body shape or size, your well-endowed wife is a finely-tuned machine — sensitive and nurturing and intuitive and feeling and powerful and delicate and complex. She and her sexuality are a deep well.

Our downfall is wanting oneness to be easy. Painless. Predictable. No wonder we're frustrated. No wonder we're angry. No wonder we're short on patience. We're completely missing the point.

> The point of marriage is not happiness. The point of marriage is growth. (Nate Bagley)

Every man becomes a detective the moment he says "I do." When wedding guests ask the groom, "Where will the two of you live?" he may as well answer, "221b Baker Street."

The chase didn't end on your wedding day — it was just getting started.

PUT IT TO WORK

1. What hints has your wife been dropping lately? What clues has she been leaving?

2. What does she need most from her husband right now? Is it empathy, encouragement, quality time, a gentle push?

3. Break a sweat until you find out.

How to Ask Her Out

I know, it doesn't sound like something we should need help with, but we do. It boils down to this:

Most of us *suck* at saying what we want.

We're indirect. We beat around the bush. We shrug our shoulders and say things like, "I dunno, whadda *you* wanna do?" In the world of women, it's viewed as soft and unattractive.

They prefer hard.

Your wife needs to hear more "I want" statements from you, plain and simple:

- "I want…"
- "I would love…"
- "It would mean a lot to me if…"
- "I would really enjoy…"

- "Here's what I'd like to do..."

- "Here's how I want to handle this..."

- "I'm in the mood for..."

It doesn't mean you disregard your wife and what she wants. It means you lead with what *you* want.

I worked with a client who was separated from his wife when he found me. After a year of working diligently on himself and the friendship with her he'd neglected for so long, the time came for him to re-introduce romance to the relationship. Here's a handful of real-life examples of how we rescripted his asks, helping him show up in his marriage as strong instead of weak:

Before: "Maybe we should be dating again." *(Weak)*

After: "I'd like to begin dating you again and rebuilding the intimate relationship we once had." *(Strong)*

Before: "Maybe you should stop in to chat." *(Weak)*

After: "I had fun tonight and don't want it to end. I'd love you to come inside so we can talk some more." *(Strong)*

Before: "My lease on the condo is up this month. What should I do?" *(Weak)*

After: "I want to move back in next month and continue repairing our relationship. How do you feel about that?" *(Strong)*

What a difference! "I want" carries strength and intention. It unleashes masculine energy and slays the passivity dragon — the silent killer that destroys so many marriages.

A DATE NIGHT REWRITE

What you're about to read is a real text from a client to his wife. I haven't embellished it for dramatic effect. Names have been changed to protect the innocent.

It's an extreme example, but notice the stark absence of anything that resembles this husband telling his wife what he wants:

> Hi honey, I know it's perhaps a last minute idea, but would you be interested in a little date tonight maybe at the beach house ... jacuzzi, wine, and a small picnic in the backyard? We could perhaps trust Amanda to babysit for a couple of hours. You won't hurt my feelings if not, so no worries either way. I just thought it might be fun to have a night without the kids. I could pick up a caprese salad and maybe chicken piccata to-go from Gianni's and you could relax with wine and your other guilty pleasure (cigarettes). We don't even need to do it right away. We could go over later around 7:30 or even 8:00. Just let me know what you think. I love you.

I need a shower.

130 words. Pure drivel. But hopefully it drives the point home: You and I need to grow some backbones, stand tall, and tell our wives what we *want!*

I said to him, "Your text sounds more like an apology than an invitation. What do you *want?* I've read it twice, and honestly, I can't tell."

Here's my rewrite. I pared it down to 35 words:

> I'd love some alone time with you tonight. I'm thinking jacuzzi, wine, caprese salad, and chicken piccata at the beach house. I checked with Amanda and she's available to babysit. How does 8:00 sound?

My email to him the next day read in part:

> Eliminate all weak, passive, indirect, wishy-washy language from your conversations and texts. No more *might, perhaps, maybe, no worries either way,* or *I just thought.* CRUSH AND KILL IT ALL!

> Instead, use phrases like, *It would be a blast! I've been thinking about you all day, We'll have so much fun, I can't wait to see you, I'll take care of a babysitter,* and *Doesn't that sound relaxing?*

> Let's move toward strong, direct, bold, unapologetic, positive, inviting, and concise! Beth is a bottom-liner and needs you to get to the point *much* quicker.

WE'RE ALL GUILTY

Yes, it's an extreme example, but I hear an abbreviated version of it daily from the men I coach! There's one phrase, more than any other, I have to work really hard to remove from the vocabulary (and subconscious) of *all* my clients. Five little words that nauseate our wives and reveal our collective emasculation:

"If you want, we could..."

- "If you want, we could do something."

- "If you want, we could watch a show."

- "If you want, we could go somewhere."

- "If you want, we could order out."

- "If you want, we could cut off my remaining testicle."

It would be funny if it weren't so close to the truth.

I hope seeing these words in print turns your stomach and helps you recognize how weak, mealy-mouthed, and unattractive they are. We want to *entice* your wife, not make her yawn.

Notice how different these words feel. Down in your gut:

- "I'd like to spend some time with you this weekend. Are you available Friday night?"

- "I'd love to curl up on the couch with you tonight. You pick the movie and I'll grab some food on my way home."

- "You know what I want to do this Saturday? Take you out for breakfast. How about that little café you love on Fountain?"

PUT IT TO WORK

1. Using what you've learned, ask your wife out this weekend.

2. Pour gasoline over "If you want, we could ..." and light a match to it. *Never* utter those words again.

3. Use an "I want" statement instead.

No more hinting.

No more beating around the bush.

Be direct.

Say what you want.

The Dopamine Advantage

*Resist the old. The predictable. The familiar. It leads to more
of the same. Follow the yellow brick road instead.*

—BORKO

Understanding the yin and yang of healthy, intimate, long-term
relationships is vital to our success as men. First, I'll summarize
the yin. Your marriage needs high levels of these three things:

1. Predictability

2. Routine

3. Sameness

It means your spouse can count on you to <u>fill in the blank</u> — go to
work when you're supposed to go to work, be home when you say
you'll be home, pay the bills on time, clean the kitchen while she
bathes the kids, and lock up the house before bed.

The result?

Strong, underlying feelings of trust and security. No surprise
there. This part we understand.

Here's the part we don't. Your marriage needs *equally* high levels of these three things:

1. Unpredictability

2. Novelty

3. Newness

It's why your feelings for each other were so intense in the beginning — there were so many "firsts." Your first date, your first really long talk, your first kiss, your first hike up Runyon Canyon. The first time you held her hand. The first time you heard her play the piano. The first time you saw her cry or eat a bowl of cereal. It doesn't matter what it was — it was *new* and it felt amazing!

That's by design.

NEUROCHEMISTRY 101

Our brains react to novelty by dumping loads of dopamine — the feel-good neurochemical — into our systems, which compels us to want *more* of what triggered it. It's why you asked, "When can I see you again?" before you had dropped her off or kissed her goodnight. Your brain was already planning its next dopamine hit.

Wonderful, Jeff, but we're not in our 20's anymore. The thrill of first dates and budding romance is long past.

Not according to science.

Dopamine is dopamine whether you've been together a few days or a few decades.

It means you get to turn back time and create stronger feelings of attraction and closeness in your marriage by planning more "firsts" with your wife. For example:

- Take a chance and try the *other* coffee shop in town.

- Walk, bike, or hitchhike there (I'm serious).

- Pack the car for an overnight and see where the wind takes you.

- Spend a few hours at a rock-climbing gym and belay for your partner.

- Buy his & her unicycles and learn how to ride them.

- Cage dive with great whites off the coast of Gansbaai, South Africa.

From Anthropologist Helen Fisher:

Research shows that novelty — taking risks or trying something new — triggers the release of dopamine in the brain. I'm not just talking about novelty in the bedroom (although that would be a good place to start). You can get the same effect from sampling a new type of cuisine together or riding the roller coaster at an amusement park.[18]

The riskier or more unorthodox the activity, the greater the "stamp" on your brain and the greater the dopamine dump! It turbo-boosts the bond with your spouse, creates more good feelings between you, and produces richer, longer-term memories of your shared experience.

Dopamine for the trifecta!

It all adds up to this:

Not all quality time is created equal. Novelty counts for more. Weird counts for more. *"That was insane!"* counts for a *lot* more.

So let "consistent," "dependable," and "regular" describe your commitment to your family and the rhythm of your bowel movements, but when it comes to planning quality time with your wife, put a knife to the throat of same ol', same ol' and try something new. Go rogue. Surprise her.

Building a strong and sexy marriage takes work.

The latest research shows it also takes play.

UP YOUR YANG

1. Break ranks with routine, surprise your wife, and do something worth remembering this week! Think *new*, *novel*, and *off-the-beaten-path*.

2. Over coffee or cocktails, make a list of things you could do together for the first time.

3. Pick one, plan it, and do it.

4. Repeat.

Confession: Three Ways I Abused Sex with My Wife

You think strong men are dangerous? Wait till you see what weak men are capable of.

—JORDAN B. PETERSON

Your view of sex probably needs a makeover. Mine sure did. I was dysfunctional on a number of levels. In step with this book's theme of running *toward* discomfort, here are the three ways I abused sex in my marriage:

1. I USED SEX TO SELF-SOOTHE

In other words, I didn't need my wife there. Oh, it was wonderful having her there, but it wasn't an *us* moment. It was a *me* moment. I got mine. That's what mattered.

How degrading.

Toward the end, sex became too painful even for me. As many men discover, there *is* something worse than not having sex, and that's having sex with a woman who looks like she'd rather be doing *anything* else.

A client on the verge of losing his marriage told me, "I was fine with my wife not enjoying sex. Sad, right? It was obvious she was just going through the motions. We were having sex, but it was robotic. She stopped looking at me. She stopped kissing me. Months before she called it quits, she would close her eyes and cover her breasts while we made love. *Why did I think that was OK?! Why didn't I care enough to find out why?!* What an idiot. What a selfish prick. She was waving red flags in my face — *literally in my face!* — and I chose not to see them."

He went on to say, "Tell the men you write for, 'Guys, take this seriously. Don't turn a blind eye! If your wife is going through the motions, your house is on fire. You'll lose everything unless you wake up! And you need to do more than schedule a date night. Call a therapist. Reach out to Jeff. Get help. But whatever you do, don't wait! *Do it now!* '"

Yeah, what he said.

2. I USED SEX AS A BAROMETER

Even when our relationship was in obvious decline, I told myself, "Well, we're still having sex 2-3 times a week. Everything must be OK. I mean, *I'm* happy."

Is it any surprise that one of the biggest reasons women stop making love to their husbands is they're afraid of sending the wrong message? In a 2012 survey, "Why Wives Say No to Sex," one out of five said they withhold sex because their husbands misinterpret lovemaking to mean everything is OK in the relationship.[19]

In his mind, sex is her stamp of approval on him and his sorry-ass contribution to their marriage, even if she's closing her eyes and covering her breasts! Somehow he still hears, "We're good. I'm happy with the way things are. Keep doing what you're doing, hot stuff. Don't change a thing. Our marriage is everything I dreamed it would be."

No! Unenthused sex with your wife *doesn't* mean everything is OK. It's the exact opposite! She's trying to get your attention. What RoboWife is really saying when she withholds sex or lets you use her vagina to masturbate is, "No, we're *not* good! I'm *not* happy with the way things are! I don't feel close to you. I don't feel connected to you. This isn't working for me anymore. We need help!"

Her Ground Proximity Warning System is blaring, "TOO LOW! TOO LOW! TERRAIN! TERRAIN! PULL UP! PULL UP!"

It's easy to talk a big game leading up to sex, but afterward, when the tension is over (temporarily, at least), most of us revert to complacency. If we regard sex as proof everything's OK, our wives withhold sex as proof it's *not*.

The wife of a client cautioned him, "You're using one yardstick to measure our marriage — *and it's the wrong one.*"

So yeah, sex is a really bad barometer.

Here's a much better one:

Do you and your wife feel closer and more connected to each other today than you did yesterday?

Hang *that* one on the wall.

3. I USED SEX TO FEEL CLOSE TO MY WIFE

Huh?! Isn't that the point?!

On one hand, yes. Sex releases a cocktail of chemical messengers throughout our brains and bodies, and many are designed to promote feelings of closeness and intimacy with our partners.

That's the point.

But...

It's not a substitute for doing the things that make for a close and intimate marriage!

Sex is supposed to be a celebration — an outward expression of the closeness and intimacy that already exists between partners. It's supposed to heighten the feelings of safety, security, acceptance, delight, and deep connection already present in your marriage. To reinforce the emotional bonds already in place.

Sex was a cheap way for me to momentarily *feel* like I had a great marriage, instead of manning up, running toward discomfort, and actually *building* a great marriage.

MASSIVE difference.

If your "lovemaking" even slightly resembles what I've described above, you're in serious danger of losing a lot more than sex. It's time to go beast mode.

> Change before you have to. (Jack Welch)

PUT IT TO WORK

1. First, get really honest and ask yourself: "Is my wife going through the motions during sex? And if so, why is that OK?" Sit with this one for a while.

2. Or maybe you're using sex as a barometer. That's where these strong, intimacy-building questions from my first book come in. Turn off the TV early tonight and ask your wife one or two of them:

   - What's most challenging about being married to me?

   - Where do you feel short-changed in our relationship?

   - Finish the sentence: "I wish my husband..."

   - If you were to give me one piece of marriage advice, what would it be?

   - Is there anything I devote regular time to that you see as a possible threat to our marriage?

   - What's one fun thing you wish we did more of?

- Are you happy with my work schedule? What would you change?

- What's your biggest concern about our relationship?

- What would you change about how we manage our money?

- What do you miss most about the early days of our relationship?

- What's something you've explained to me before, but in your opinion, I'm just not getting it — you still don't feel heard or understood?

- If you could change one thing about our priorities as a family, what would it be?

3. Ask yourself: "Has sex become a substitute for doing the inconvenient and uncomfortable things that make for a close and intimate relationship? Am I using it to mask bigger issues and momentarily *feel* like I have a great marriage, instead of doing the hard work of actually *building* a great marriage?"

4. If so, address those bigger issues. Charge into them headfirst. But don't do it alone. Invite accountability. Confide in your band of brothers. Find a mentor or hire a coach.

And get back to building a better marriage.

Today.

Dear Men

*No other man can replace you in your life. You are the hero in
your story. Not a bit player, not an extra, but the main man.*[20]

—JOHN ELDREDGE

This letter is written by a woman. A very wise and compassionate
one. Shadé Ashani is a mentor, healer, breakthrough coach,
philanthropist, and author of *In Search of My Father*. Her mission
is to bring an end to the unnecessary suffering caused by our
stories of unworthiness.

I'm grateful for her work and her permission to include this ode.
Equal parts painful and hopeful, I know it will speak to you.

Dear Men,

We miss you.

Deeply.

When women gather together in circles, we tell stories of how much we long for you. Crave you. Pray for you to rise and meet us here. We mourn your missing presence. In our childhoods. In the homes we've built without you. In our beds.

We hold hands and beg God to set you free from whatever keeps you from standing at our sides. Right here.

Here in intimacy.

In integrity.

In wholeness.

In freedom.

The places where you are caught in dishonesty, shame, fear, addiction — we grieve and rage over.

We see your pain and we see your power.

We miss you.

We love you.

We can't wait for you to come Home.

For the men who have, thank you so much. Please call your brothers, start men's circles, show them the manuals. Tell them of what you gave up. Of your brokenness and acceptance. Of what it truly means to take up the mantle of protector. Please. There aren't enough fathers, resources, and leaders for men to sit at the feet of.

The women have tried. We can't do it. The restoration must come from within the Masculine. The Feminine cannot mother grown men into wholeness. We cannot strap men to our backs and walk.

We tried.

We bow out. Not gracefully. But in mournful acceptance nonetheless.

And we will wait for you to burst free from the shackles patriarchy has placed on you.

We pray.

We pray.

We pray.

For the Great Remembrance.

–Shadé Ashani

CONTACT SHADÉ

- Website: shadeashani.com
- Instagram: @shade.ashani
- Email: hello@shadeashani.com

Eyes Wide Shut

Nothing in a relationship ever gets better on its own. You might as well ask the ingredients in your pantry to bake themselves into a cake.

−JEN GUNTER

We'll come back to this chapter's opening quote in a minute, but first, a quick story about my car...

A few days before my last oil change and tune-up, my car's check engine light came on. Good timing, right?

It ended up being a minor issue — easily fixed — but my mechanic forgot to clear the diagnostic trouble code from my car's computer, which meant the check engine light was still on. I called him a few hours later and he said, "My bad. Swing by when you're in the area and I'll reset that for you."

No big deal.

It was such a "No big deal" that I didn't make time for it.

Days turned into weeks (as they do) and weeks turned into months (as they do), and my very efficient brain did exactly what it's *programmed* to do: It moved that pesky red light into the background and filed it between the fingerprint marks on our front door and the dust on top of our bathroom vanity lights that I don't see anymore.

Essentially, my brain made the check engine light invisible. I stopped seeing the very thing — *Hey! Look at me! Over here! Something's wrong!* — that was designed to get my attention.

Sounds like my marriage.

I ignored my wife's red flags for so long, they stopped being red flags. My brain blended them into the background and I stopped seeing them altogether.

Every client I've ever worked with has echoed something similar. "I saw the warning signs but didn't do anything. I ignored them."

Label it however you'd like — proud, arrogant, careless, irresponsible, foolish, short-sighted, weak, fragile, or dumb as shit — but the result is the same: Things don't get better, they get worse. Our marriages die a slow death.

Last Saturday we laid to rest a 52-year-old family friend. Five beautiful children. A net worth in the tens of millions. The second half of his life waiting to be lived. A few years ago, his doctor tried to get his attention: "Stop drinking or you won't see your youngest graduate from middle school."

He responded, "I'll get on that."

He didn't.

THE OTHER "V" WORD

I'm known for helping husbands save their marriages, but that's not actually what I do. What I *actually* do is help them become great men. The kind of men their wives could grow to respect, admire, and adore one day. As James Clear writes, "Improvements are only temporary until they become part of who you are."[21] Identity is everything! We know who you've *been* (and see the results), but who do you want to *become?*

I've posed that question to hundreds of guys, and their answers wouldn't surprise you. The words they choose — strong, passionate, laser-focused, generous, teachable, confident, leader, learner, warrior — are probably similar to the words you would choose.

But here's one thing that *is* surprising...

In all my years of helping men forge new identities, no one has ever chosen the word "vigilant." Not even in Christendom, where it's elevated to super-star status.

vig·i·lant | vi'-jə-lənt | adjective

1. On high alert, especially to detect possible danger

2. Watchful; attentive to avoid danger or to provide safety; circumspect; cautious; wary

Up early. Inspecting the fences around the perimeter of your property. Climbing the watchtower, scanning the horizon, and investigating every possible threat. Taking swift action when you smell danger. Getting in touch with the fiercer side of your nature. Using every weapon at your disposal to protect your marriage and family.

It's a central part of every husband's calling. As deep-rooted as our sex drives.

MISPLACED OPTIMISM

Look again at the quote we opened with:

Nothing in a relationship ever gets better on its own.

Ever.

I didn't believe this 10 years ago. I wanted to, but my optimism kept getting in the way:

- "We'll be fine."

- "Deep down, we love each other."

- "Things will get better somehow."

Looking back, it wasn't optimism at all. It was passivity *disguised* as optimism. Here's how you can tell the difference:

Optimism says, "Not only can we work through this, but we'll have a closer and more intimate marriage on the other side. Let's get some help. We're worth it!"

Passivity says, "We'll be fine. I'll give my marriage the attention it needs as soon as things slow down at the office."

Optimism sounds the alarm and takes action. Passivity crosses its fingers and watches the building burn down.

May I suggest a new strategy?

Do one thing today to move in your spouse's direction. To bring sexy back. To make your marriage a priority again. Not two things, not three things. Just one.

Write her a note. Or plan a date night. Or uncross your fingers and message me. Time doesn't heal wounds. It's actually Miracle Grow® for unaddressed issues in your marriage.

PUT IT TO WORK

1. Add vigilance to the top of your "Qualities I Must Develop in Order to be a Kick-Ass Husband" list.

2. Exchange your belief in magic for belief in cause and effect.

3. Ask yourself: "Is my marriage in trouble or about to be? What warning signs have I been ignoring?"

4. Ask yourself: "Do I suffer from misplaced optimism? What's one thing I can do *right now* to change course and build a better marriage?"

Get on that!

If you don't change direction, you'll end up where you're heading. (Lao Tzu)

The Two Greatest Threats to Your Manhood & Marriage

Everything worthwhile is uphill. Everything.

–JOHN MAXWELL

None of us enjoy conflict. None of us enjoy arguing or fighting with our spouse. But in my experience, there's something much worse than a fight, and that's a fight with no resolution.

1. We go to our separate corners.

2. We check out emotionally — either with busywork or social media.

3. We ignore each other.

In the immortal words of Dr Phil, "How's that workin' for ya?"

BREAK THE CYCLE

I do more than encourage and advise my clients, I help them become badass. I developed a roadmap to get there called "The

7 Core Commitments." A potential client must agree to embrace and embody all seven or there's no point in us working together. I'm happy to send you a copy, but today I want to pull a few bullet points from Core Commitment #4 (Bold Initiative):

- Strong husbands make the first move.

- Strong husbands make the second move.

- We step into the spaces we used to avoid.

- We don't wait for opportunity, we *create* it.

That's very different from the way I behaved most of my married life. I was a chronic avoider. Guys, nothing does more damage to a relationship than avoidance! It's not the fight. It's not the disagreement. It's not the misunderstanding...

It's the distance. It's the separation. It's the deafening silence.

I spoke with someone last week who wants my help breaking the cycle that's been in his marriage for decades. I asked him, "What's the cycle?"

He explained, "She says something critical... I defend myself... she gets upset because I didn't hear her... I get frustrated because she's overreacting... then we go to opposite ends of the house and avoid each other for a few days."

Stepping into the spaces we used to avoid means when she goes to her corner, you *don't* go to yours. You go after her. You go find her.

I'm going to tell you how to do that — including what to say and what not to say — but first, let's square off against the two greatest threats to closeness and intimacy when there's tension or unresolved conflict in your home.

THREAT #1: SILENCE

Silence is the enemy. Here's why: In the silence of disconnection and hurt feelings and going to your separate corners, your wife's inner critic is running his mouth off.

If her "opposite end of the house" is your master bedroom, she's not alone in that bedroom. Her inner critic is whispering something like this:

> "Damn, girl. This is *not* what you signed up for. You two are more like roommates than soulmates. Let's face it, the spark is gone. And if you're honest with yourself, it's been gone for years. *Can we please admit that now?!* I mean, really, aren't you tired of this? Tired of feeling alone in your marriage? It sucks. Especially when there are so many good men out there! Men who would love you and pay attention to you. Hmmm, what about Fabio? You and he had something really special back in the day. I bet he'd love to hear from you. Get on Facebook and see what he's up to. Your husband? Pfffttt ... like he'd care. He only notices you when he wants sex."

Advantage, Fabio.

You might be giving your wife the silent treatment, but her inner critic isn't. He's an opportunist. You sulking and staying away from your spouse is his opportunity to defile your marriage. To drive a deeper wedge between you.

THREAT #2: WAITING

Waiting is the enemy. Being passive is the enemy. Marriages don't get better in limbo. They only deteriorate. They only get worse.

The truth is — after a fight with no resolution — *your wife* is the one who's waiting. She's waiting for you to pursue her. To come after her. She *wants* you to come after her. It's part of her DNA.

It's one of the biggest mistakes I made in my marriage. I interpreted my wife's silence or anger or emotional distance as cues to give her space. To stay away. To leave her alone. I found out later I was dead wrong. *She wanted me to come after her!*

One of my closest friends — his name is Jonathan — owns a gutter business. During a lunch break one Friday, his foreman, Scott, shared the story of a fight he and his wife had the night before. The fight ended when Scott's wife stormed out of the room, ran upstairs, and slammed their bedroom door.

That week Jonathan was reading my first book and said, "That's so crazy! I'm reading a book written by a friend, and I just finished a chapter called 'Women and the Fine Art of Door Slamming.' It's about what to do in that exact situation!"

Naturally, Scott asked, "Well, what does he say?"

"He says you're supposed to go after her. He says your wife is on the other side of that door *waiting* for you to come after her."

Scott replied, "Uh, no offense to your friend, but that's about the dumbest thing I've ever heard. There's *no way* she wanted me to come after her. [snicker] I guarantee it."

Monday rolled around, and Scott approached Jonathan and said, "You're not gonna believe what my wife said this morning. Let me back up ... We had that fight, right? Well, we avoided each other all weekend. It totally sucked. The ice finally started to thaw yesterday afternoon. So before leaving for work today, I asked her, 'Last week when we had that big blow up, and you ran upstairs and slammed our bedroom door ... you weren't waiting for me to come after you, were you? I know, it's a stupid question, but my boss is reading this marriage book and the author says you were hoping I'd come after you. Were you?'"

His wife answered, "Buy the book. That's *exactly* what I was hoping you'd do."

Remember, it's part of her DNA. She's waiting for you to come find her. Do *not* wait for her to come find you! YOU ARE NOT THE PRINCESS. Masculine energy pursues. Masculine energy leaves the safety of the shore. Masculine energy is warrior and protector. If connection — if intimacy — has been broken, it's your job to get it back. It's your job to be strong.

Now let's move from theory to practice (on your way to mastery) with two testosterone-boosting action steps. Consider the next few pages the extended "Put It to Work" section of this chapter.

1. GET UP AND GO FIND HER

Leave where you are and go to where she is. It's simple physics. If she's in the bedroom with the door closed, open the door and walk into the bedroom. If she's reclining on a chaise lounge in your backyard, go to the backyard, pull up a chair, and sit next to her.

Just *move*.

Because subconsciously your wife is always asking:

- "Will he pursue me — not just when it's easy — but when it's hard?"

- "Will he love me even when I act unlovable?"

- "When my hormones are a runaway train?"

- *"Am I worth it?"*

Going after her says, "Yes, you're worth it." Avoiding her says, "No, you're not." Not answering her question isn't an option! You're *always* answering it — through your action or inaction.

So get up. And go find her.

2. BREAK THE SILENCE

This is imperative: You speak first. You be the one to break the silence. It's not enough to go after her. You be the first one to open your mouth.

Quick qualifier — don't start with a question:

- "Hey, where'd you go?" is another form of avoidance. You went and found her, but now let's avoid the issue and sweep it under the rug.

- "Are you upset?" is better but way too soft. Of course she's upset!

- "Why are you so cold and distant?" is passive-aggressive. You might as well ask, "Why are you acting like such a crazy, unreasonable bitch?"

Don't ask her anything! Opening with a question is just a cleverly disguised way of saying, "I'm not comfortable leading this marriage. You lead, honey. I'll follow."

No! Own the moment! You started strong. You made the first move. You left your comfort zone and went after her. Now *finish* strong. Find her, get in her space, and say:

"There's distance between us, and I'm *not* OK with it."

That's gold! Write that down. Then acknowledge and own your part of whatever went south between you two (see "Apologize Like a Man," page 34).

But Jeff, what if I don't know what went south between us?

You may not. That's the point. Find out! Go after her and say:

> "I really enjoyed dinner with you tonight. You know, we were clearing the table and something happened. I'm not sure what exactly, but now there's distance between

us. I should probably know what caused it... I don't. But I *want* to know, because no one's more important to me than you. Nothing's more important to me than *us*. So, can you help me? What did I miss down there?"

That's when she says, "You had me at hello. You had me the moment I looked up and saw you walking toward me like a man on a mission. Like a prince coming for his princess."

Don't do what I did! I squandered my marriage and fractured my family because I was passive. When there was distance between us, I played the princess. I waited. I did nothing.

And what my wife heard was, "Yeah, there's distance between us. Yeah, there's tension in our home. And you know what? I really don't care. I've got more important things to worry about. More important things to take care of."

You know what else she heard?

"I'm not coming after you. You're not worth fighting for." That is *not* the message you want to send your wife.

Ever.

So get up and go find her. That's the hero move. Break the silence. Fumble through it if you have to. It doesn't matter! Her respect for you will go through the roof. *Your* respect for you will go through the roof.

Step into the spaces you used to avoid and watch the difference it makes.

Sticky Situations

The cave you fear to enter holds the treasure you seek.
−JOSEPH CAMPBELL

Do you know who Dr. John Gottman is?

Long revered for his work on love, marriage, and divorce prediction, Gottman's writings are considered the gold standard of the industry. He's done extensive research with thousands of couples inside his Love Lab at the University of Washington. 40 years worth. Here's something he said that got my attention:

> More than 80% of the time, it's the wife who brings up sticky marital issues, while the husband tries to avoid discussing them.[22]

More than 80% of the time.

That's insane!

That means...

- When life says, "Time to step up. Time to bring your

best. Time to run *toward* Goliath," we shrink instead.

- When life screams, *"Growth moment,"* we ignore the invitation to grow and get better. We sidestep responsibility and run to the gym or go back to playing video games.

- When life asks, "Who wears the pants in this family?" we shake our heads from side to side and silently mouth, "Not me," then point at our wives.

So yes, there's a man in the house, but she's not very well-suited for the job. Oh, she'll do it, but she'll resent you for it.

She'd much rather trade places. She'd much rather soften and fill the home with her *feminine* energy. She'd much rather follow your lead.

Gottman, again:

> More than 80% of the time it's the wife who brings up sticky marital issues, while the husband tries to avoid discussing them.[23]

In my home, it hovered near the 100% mark.

Here's what avoiding important conversations — *conversations that could have changed the course of my marriage and life!* — said to the woman I shared a bed with:

- "Honesty … intimacy … connection? Nah, I'm good."

- "I'd rather stay small than grow and build a better

marriage. I'd rather *pretend* everything is OK than have to face my inadequacies as a husband."

- "In the story I'm writing, you don't matter. Get used to not being a priority around here."

- "I'm careful about working out and eating right, but I'm willing to roll the dice in our marriage."

- "What's the problem? We're having sex twice a week. *I'm* happy."

It's hard to believe, but I actually used to think, "Huh … I wonder why isn't she attracted to me anymore?"

[face palm]

IDENTITY: ~~AVOIDER~~ INITIATOR

> Our biggest successes are born out of discomfort, uncertainty, and risk.[24] (Gary John Bishop)

OK, let's tap into your masculine energy stores. They might be buried beneath years of neglect, but like the ring of power in Tolkien's tales of Middle Earth, your masculinity *wants* to be found. It's trying to get back to its master.

This week, use the element of surprise to your advantage. Bring up a sticky marital issue after you've put some thought into it and have a solution to present. Something like this:

> "I've been thinking about us this week. I've been thinking about how important you are to me. The last

time you brought up [the issue], I fed you a bunch of one-word answers and tried to avoid the topic. I only made it worse, didn't I?

"Yeah, I thought so. Here's what I'm thinking: From now on when [the issue happens], I will [proposed solution that helps your wife feel loved and cherished].

"How does that sound to you?"

Or maybe it doesn't call for an immediate solution. You can still strengthen your marriage simply by being the one who brings it up!

Yes, I said that. You can still strengthen your marriage simply by being the one who brings it up!

Remember, this is about leadership, *not* about having it all figured out. So instead of presenting a solution, ask your wife to help you understand how she feels about the issue at hand. That's the all-important part most of us miss anyway.

Something like this:

"I've been thinking about us this week. I've been thinking about how important you are to me. The last time you brought up [the issue], I fed you a bunch of one-word answers and tried to avoid the topic. I only made it worse, didn't I?

"Yeah, I thought so. I'm obviously missing something. Would you help me understand how [the issue] makes you feel. I'm sure you've told me before, but tell me again. I'm ready to listen this time. I want to know how you feel."

Welcome to SEAL Team Six.

FLIP IT!

Imagine if you flipped Gottman's 80/20 on its head!

Imagine if *you* were the one to bring up sticky marital issues 80% of the time compared to your wife's 20%. Imagine the marriage you'd have. Imagine the man you'd become!

But Jeff, I suck at this stuff.

You used to suck at riding a bike, too. We all did! This isn't something you'll become proficient at overnight. It might be *months* before you remove the training wheels. Just get started!

> Fear is not the enemy. Waiting to stop feeling afraid is.[25]
> (Marie Forleo)

Fear is OK.

Anxiety is OK.

Fumbling over your words is OK.

But standing still *isn't!*

Handing the leadership baton to your wife isn't!

Avoiding important discussions and leaving the health of your marriage to chance isn't!

Keep moving toward discomfort, uncertainty, and things you suck at. Revel in it! It's what we're made for. You'll build credibility with yourself *and* with your wife.

PUT IT TO WORK

1. Use my script as a guide.

2. Fill in the blanks. Write out what you want to say.

3. Say it.

Refer to your notes and read them if you have to. I'm serious! Your wife won't care! On the contrary, she'll be moved. She'll be beaming. She'll be drawn to you.

Her husband is putting his ego aside and caring for her heart.

Her husband is leading the charge toward a closer and more intimate marriage.

Her husband has his pants back on.

For now :)

This Chapter Will Save You *Lots* of Time[26]

The short-term pain of accepting a truth is much better than the long-term pain of believing an illusion.

−LILKA

I hate to do this because it cheapens the rest of the book, but I'm offering you a shortcut, one that will fast-track you to the front of the line. One that will give you instant access to all the sex you could possibly imagine. One that will allow you to bypass everything we've talked about so far — all the hard work, all the commitment, all the sacrifice — and still get the girl.

First, I need your word you'll keep this between us. Don't share what I'm about to reveal with the guys who haven't read this far. And get ready to toss this useless piece of crap in the trash. You won't be needing it.

Here it is — the tested and proven shortcut that makes the rest of this book obsolete. Two words:

Use porn.

Yes, use porn. It will make you a better man, give you what you want, and even resolve your intimacy issues. Plus, it's quick and easy.

All of that is true, of course, except for the part about making you a better man, giving you what you want, and resolving your intimacy issues.

AN INCONVENIENT TRUTH

I recently perused the really cool website of an organization that relies on science and fact, not morality, to educate people about the harmful effects of pornography. It was launched by a handful of college students out of Utah. I love their approach, I dig what they do, I already mentioned the website, but it's their name that caught my attention: *Fight the New Drug.*

Porn, a drug? I realize it can be addictive for some, but... *a drug?* Really, young hipsters, I think you're overreaching. Drugs are what we use to relieve stress. Or numb pain. Or escape a reality we feel powerless to change. Drugs are how we create a fantasy world where nothing is required of us. Or demanded of us. Where everything is just the way we... *whoops*, never mind.

Our relationship with porn might change if we viewed it the way we view heroin. Or Celebrex. At least prescription drug companies are required by law to present the benefits and risks of their products "in a balanced fashion." And ya gotta tip your hat to 'em, because they do it spectacularly well. Their TV advertisements depict attractive and energetic people smiling, horseplaying, and sharing tender moments. Their homes are modern and immaculately kept. The scenes are so magical (even the teenagers are smiling), you'll hardly notice when the soothing voiceover transitions from the drug's benefits to risks. I transcribed this one word-for-word from an actual commercial:

> This medication may cause serious allergic reactions or suicidal thoughts or actions. Tell your doctor right away if you have these: new or worsening depression, unusual changes in mood or behavior, or swelling of the face, mouth, lips, gums, tongue, throat, or neck; trouble breathing, rash, hives, blisters, muscle pain with fever, tired feeling, or blurry vision. Common side effects are dizziness, sleepiness, weight gain, and swelling of the hands, legs, and feet.

May cause ... *suicidal actions?! Are they serious?!* You mean like walking in front of a train or putting a gun in my mouth? If only the porn industry was forced to be this honest. Imagine if every trip down Porn Lane was prefaced by:

> What you're about to view is more potent than high-grade heroin and faster in its onset of action. It will hijack your brain's reward center, carving new and dangerous neural pathways, which, in turn, will render you incapable of forming close and satisfying relationships. In lieu of a happy ending, you'll be left feeling even more frustrated, hollow, and unfulfilled.

> Evidence suggests porn will not solve your problems at home, but likely exacerbate them and create new

ones. Pornographic use is shown to increase marital tension and discord, erode trust, destroy intimacy, and heighten feelings of resentment. Even a strong marriage cannot compete with the unnatural and artificial levels of chemical excitement porn offers. Men who indulge rate themselves as less in love with their partner, less attracted to their partner, less satisfied with their partner, and more critical of their partner's appearance. They also cite greater frequency of erectile dysfunction, premature ejaculation, and involuntary outbursts of road rage. Spouses report feelings of loss, betrayal, mistrust, devastation, and anger. Many exhibit symptoms of anxiety and depression, with an increase in suicidal thoughts and actions.

Porn, like all medications, carries some risk of dependency. Get help right away if you have these: new or worsening insecurity, unusual changes in sexual preferences, emotional detachment, lack of empathy toward your spouse, sleeplessness, chronic self-loathing, unrealistic expectations in marriage, or a tendency to objectify women. Common side effects include denial, self-centeredness, isolation, shorter attention span, decreased productivity, and carpal tunnel syndrome. Studies show that married men who look at porn are more likely to cheat on their wives, visit prostitutes, confuse sex with love, and trade time with their children for time alone in a dark room. In some cases, repeated exposure to pornography leads to sexual compulsion, sexual addiction, sexual assault, divorce, loss of employment, and soullessness.

Individual results may vary.

The world you're about to enter isn't real. It erroneously depicts the fairer sex as subordinate and less-than-human, nothing more than objects to be used and consumed. The women on your screen are actresses — wind-up dolls surgically enhanced, airbrushed, and photoshopped for your sexual pleasure. They don't actually *enjoy* being exploited, manhandled, abused, hit, yelled at, humiliated, and otherwise mistreated. It's make-believe. A distortion. What you *will* see in this fictional online world are smiling and seductive faces. What you *won't* see are the grimaces, STDs, intestinal parasites, cervical cancer, bruises, torn skin, mounds of bloody tissues, anal and vaginal surgical repairs, unwanted pregnancies, abortions, or the teenage girl crying alone off camera.

The majority of these "stars" were sexually abused as children. A handful were lured into porn under false pretenses and subsequently kidnapped, threatened, beaten, and raped in order to crush their spirit. (Some of the material you're about to view contains actual footage of their indoctrination.) We coerce and even force our actresses to do things that are dehumanizing. It's the reason 75% of them numb themselves with drugs or alcohol prior to filming.

Enjoy!

And that's the sanitized version.

LIVE FREE

I like looking at pictures of naked women, but I'd much rather get my hands on a real one. It's the reason I stay away from porn. It's not because I'm a saint, it's because I've read the fine print.

Porn is a colossal rip-off.

It's also a powerful and addictive drug, one that will grind *you* to powder. If porn has been one-upping you lately, I've got some really good news:

1. You're not alone

2. Help is just a mouse-click away

You can find it at xxxchurch.com. I've known the staff up close for 15 years, and they're some of the most caring, down-to-earth people I know. Through workshops, small groups, accountability software, and online community, they help ordinary Joes (and Josephines) find freedom from porn. *Live Free* is their app and private online community for men, and since its launch in 2019, I've had the privilege of serving as its resident Marriage Coach. At $5 a month, it's the best investment you'll ever make. Say hello if you decide to give it a test drive (livefree.app).

Life is better without porn.

Marriage is better without porn.

Sex is better without porn.

You're better without porn.

"I Love You, but I'm Not *in Love* with You"

No man is more unhappy than he who never faces
adversity. For he's not permitted to prove himself.

−SENECA

A husband on Long Island got the i-love-you-but-i'm-no-longer-*in-love*-with-you talk from his wife. Desperate not to lose his family, he bought my first book, devoured it, and BOOM! — the scales fell from his eyes. That same week he called asking for advice. What you're about to read is part of my conversation with him.

Those aren't easy words to hear, but know this: Deep down, this isn't what she wants. What she *wants* is to be madly in love with her husband. What she *wants* is to swoon over you. What she *wants* is a close and intimate marriage. It's why she immerses herself in television shows like *The Bachelorette* and *This Is Us*.

"I love you, but I'm not *in love* with you," is a defense mechanism.

It's her way of saying, "If you won't protect and care for my heart, I'll do it myself."

It's what women with absentee husbands do.

My three suggestions:

1. PLAY THE LONG GAME

Yes, you mean business. Yes, you're for real. And yes, your wife wants to believe you're for real. It's true! But there's a war raging deep inside her. Bells and whistles might be going off inside *your* head, but a prosecutor is leveling charges against you inside hers:

> "Well, we've heard *this* before. Like those tears are real. Ha! Yeah, right. Who's his acting coach? He must think you're a flaming fool. Remember the last time this happened? The last time he promised things would be different? You fell for it and had your heart broken all over again. Are you really that stupid? Are you really that pathetic? Don't you *dare* let him back in! *For what?!* So you can feel invisible and alone again?! So you can go back to being roommates?! I'm warning you... YOU WILL NEVER FORGIVE YOURSELF!"

It's dark in there, believe me.

Have you ever watched a sunrise? The sky isn't jet black one moment then brilliant the next. The darkness rolls back *slowwwly*. Dawn isn't an arena rock song, it's a symphony in four movements. Truth takes root in our hearts the same way.

So let her warm up to you incrementally. Over time. On her own terms. Even if it takes longer than what you deem "fair." Pressuring her will only strengthen the accusations in her head against you.

Which would you prefer: a weak, reluctant, half-baked commitment because you twisted her arm (and a firestorm of resentment the first time you do something careless or selfish) or a strong, resolute, all-in commitment because she refused to betray her conscience, stood at a safe distance, waited to see if you were for real, wrestled honestly with her doubts, observed you some more, then decided *for herself* to let you back in?

2. MAKE THIS JOURNEY ABOUT YOU, NOT HER

Make it about *you* becoming a better husband, a better person, a better man. If it's about *her* and her response — "I'm changing but she won't acknowledge it," or "I gave her flowers but got nothing in return," or "I complimented her but she didn't compliment me back" — this will all be a BIG waste of time. Cross these off your list or you won't last a week:

- I need my wife to acknowledge me.

- I need my wife to respond to me.

- I need my wife to reassure me and tell me everything's going to be OK.

- I need my wife to give me praise.

Instead, treat every exchange with your wife as an opportunity. An opportunity to grow. To stretch yourself. To move past your past.

To evolve and become the hero your family is crossing its fingers for. Treat it as an opportunity to ask, "What can I do *right now* to stay the course? What can I do *right now* to earn her respect, re-establish trust, build emotional intimacy, and become a man worth following?" Let these be your guiding questions.

Believe in the latent potential of the new seeds you're planting. They won't spring up and become great trees overnight, but they *will* germinate. Something powerful is happening below the surface. More importantly, something powerful is happening inside you. No one can diminish that. No one can take that away.

Make doing the right thing and becoming a better man its own reward. If you're for real, your wife will take notice and move in your direction. We just have no control over when.

> The man who moves a mountain begins by carrying away small stones. (Confucius)

3. PROTECT HER HEART

Here's a real-life example of what it looks like to protect your wife's heart. A client of mine from Chicago was on the verge of divorce. His wife agreed to a 12-month separation knowing it would soften the blow on their children. He hired me and it was game on. A few months later, she sent him this very honest and heartfelt text, echoing what *all* women in her situation feel:

> I really want to acknowledge all your effort, but I have an inner battle raging that says I can't trust it. The skeptic in my head says you're doing it to alleviate your

own pain and not mine. I know that's not entirely fair, but considering how long it took for you to actually listen, care, and take action…what else am I supposed to think? I'm really struggling with letting my guard down.

This text I crafted was his response. I suggest memorizing it:

I get it. I'd be skeptical, too. We both know I was asleep for a long time. What if this is just for show? What if this is just a ploy to get you back? To alleviate my own pain, as you put it. You would never forgive yourself. It's waaaay too early to let your guard down. We agreed on a year of separation, and we're only a few months in. Let's give this bottle of wine time to breathe. I'm not in a hurry. I'm in this for the long haul. My goal isn't to win you back. My goal is to grow into the kind of man you could love and trust again. If and when that day comes, you'll know. It won't feel forced. Trust your intuition. I do.

In one jarringly empathetic text, he connected with his wife in nine powerful ways:

1. He sided with her.

2. He validated her feelings.

3. He comforted her.

4. He let her off the hook.

5. He acknowledged and allayed her greatest fears.

6. He gave her wings to fly back to him when she's ready.

7. He protected her heart.

8. He took responsibility for how he'd fallen short.

9. He acknowledged her experience in their marriage.

And most likely, he left her scratching her head and thinking, "Now *that's* a man I could give myself to."

We're not done. I left out the most important line of his text — the transition or "change the subject" line. It comes right after, "Trust your intuition. I do."

> I'm heading to Whole Foods. Do you need anything?

Huh?! That's the most important line?!

Yup, and here's why:

It says, "I'm not waiting for you to respond. I don't *need* you to respond. This isn't my big moment. This isn't my carefully rehearsed, put-all-my-chips-on-the-table, go-for-broke, wow-my-wife-and-get-her-to-crumble speech. No, this is my *life*. Get used to it!"

[mic drop]

Is your wife checked out? Has she hinted at divorce? Maybe she's already met with a lawyer. Most likely, you're making the same mistakes I made, and things are getting worse, not better. I created a Master Class just for you! Learn more on page 158.

How Smart Husbands Say No

Spend time with those you love. One day you'll either say:
"I wish I had," or "I'm glad I did."

—ZIG ZIGLAR

I have a new client. We'll call him Dick.

His wife, of course, is Jane.

Their marriage has a faded "OUT OF ORDER" sign taped to the front of it. Dick is a workaholic who loves his wife but can't seem to get off the hamster wheel. Jane wishes they were closer and feels like a prisoner in her own home.

A few days into our coach-client relationship, Jane invited Dick on a date. Not the "Do you have time for coffee?" kind, but the "Let's spend the day together, I've planned something fun" kind.

It included a long drive together in the car, a nice meal without the kids, deep conversation, some hand holding, and a concert under the stars at the iconic Hollywood Bowl.

Jane hinted there might even be fireworks afterward.

Here's how the rest of the conversation went:

> **Jane:** "What do you think?! *Doesn't that sound like fun?!*"
>
> **Dick:** "What day?"
>
> **Jane:** "Next Wednesday."
>
> **Dick:** "You know I can't leave the office early on a Wednesday."

Or, as she heard: "Stupid Jane, you know I can't leave the office early on a Wednesday."

Conversation over.

With a heavy heart, Jane turned and walked out of the room. But not before vowing to herself, "That's the last time I ask him to do *anything!*"

Stupid Dick.

Here's how I suggested he say no next time (if there is a next time):

> **Jane:** "What do you think?! *Doesn't that sound like fun?!*"
>
> **Dick:** "Are you kidding?! Having you all to myself for an entire evening?! That sounds *awesome!* Let me check my schedule when I get back to the office. I'll talk to my boss, shuffle a few appointments, and do everything I can to free up next Wednesday. Worst-case scenario we have to do it on a different day — but either way, it's a date! Can I let you know for sure this afternoon?"

What a difference.

True, it's not the firm commitment to next Wednesday she was hoping for, but it's certainly a firm commitment to *her* and their marriage.

Here's the problem with "I can't" or "I'm busy that day" when your spouse takes a risk and invites you to spend time with her ...

It's wide open for interpretation.

To her, "I'm busy that day" might mean:

- "You look fat."
- "I don't enjoy your company."
- "I have better things to do."
- "You don't do it for me anymore."
- "I'd rather watch paint dry."
- "You've gained weight, haven't you?"

Remember, you go to bed wondering how you'll afford the kids' college tuition. She goes to bed wondering if you're still crazy about her.

So the next time your wife asks you out, and you're pretty sure you have a prior commitment that can't be changed, say yes a dozen different ways before you say no.

Leave no room for interpretation.

Micro Moments That Make or Break Your Marriage

Masculinity is not something given to you but something you gain.
And you gain it by winning small battles with honor.

–NORMAN MAILER

Your wife complains. Or says something cryptic. Or crazy. Or hurls an unfounded accusation.

The way you respond will either make or break your marriage.

We'll start off with an easy one.

THE VEILED REQUEST

A client shared that his wife said to him, "I liked it when you used to leave me notes. I miss that." He then wondered aloud if her comment had any significance.

(I told you this was an easy one.)

Resisting the urge to hang up on him, I added, "It was an invitation.

It was her way of saying, 'When you leave me a note, I feel cherished. I feel cared for. I feel like a priority. Can you do that again?'"

An important reminder from "Embrace Your Inner Detective":

> Women don't typically come out and say what they want. After all, what's romantic about that? "Write me more notes. Or else." Boring. Any robot can issue an order. Instead, they drop a few crumbs to see if we care enough to follow the trail.

To his credit, this husband got the message. His wife's birthday is June 18th, so I suggested he leave her a card or a note on the 18th of every month — celebrating her twelve times a year instead of just one. That was ages ago and he's never missed a month.

The result?

1. She feels cherished.

2. They're closer and more intimate.

Let's go up a level.

THE HOMEMADE KOMBUCHA

A client's wife made kombucha at home for the first time. The day it was ready to drink she said, "I'm nervous about trying it." Somewhat dismissively, he replied, "That's silly. Why would you be nervous?"

It turned into a massive fight.

Why?

Seriously, what did he miss?

I said to him, "Brittany was inviting you in. She wanted to connect with you. Share a moment with you. Process her anxiety with you. Except for coaching calls like this one, men process by themselves. We *think* about the issue. But women process with others. They *talk* about the issue.

"She wasn't being silly or stupid or foolish. She was being true to her feminine self. Your disdainful reply — 'That's silly. Why would you be nervous?' — was the same as saying, 'Can't you be more like a man? I really hate your feminine side.' "

Here's how my client and I rescripted the moment:

> **Her:** "I'm nervous about trying the kombucha."
>
> **Him:** "I get it. Trying something new can be scary. What are you most nervous about?"

Colossal difference.

This is how you join her and take her side in a moment of anxiety or mild distress. This is how you build closeness and intimacy instead of eroding it.

Borrowing from Jim Collins' lexicon in *Good to Great*, we now ascend to Level Five.

THE RUINED EVENING

My client Chris and his wife Jen wrapped up a grueling workweek by enjoying some quality time together in their backyard jacuzzi. Margaritas. Intimate conversation. Laughing. And every woman's favorite oxymoron: alone together.

Their two girls were inside watching a movie when something went wonky with their cable service. Dad to the rescue!

15 minutes later Jen walked into the house.

> **Her:** "You ruined our night! You've been inside fiddling with the TV for an hour!"

> **Him:** "I don't have my watch on, but there's no way it was an hour."

Or, as Jen heard, "You don't know what the hell you're talking about. Stop acting like a spoiled brat."

RNO = Romantic Night Over

Our winning percentages go way up when we tune in to what's *not* being said by our spouse. That's because the issue being discussed or debated is seldom the real issue.

What does that mean for us?

It means the hero move is rarely on the surface. It's rarely obvious. It requires a little digging.

First, what did my client miss?

What was Jen *really* trying to say?

Here's my best guess:

> "I was looking forward to some *us* time tonight. Life is busy and moments like these are rare. You left me out there by myself for what felt like an eternity. My insecurities got the best of me and I started to think, 'Maybe he's not interested in spending time with me.' Is that true, honey?"

Remember, the issue isn't the actual issue. The problem isn't the actual problem. It's something deeper. In this case, the real issue wasn't how long Chris was inside trying to get the TV to work. The real issue was Jen felt abandoned, alone, and unimportant.

The strong move, therefore, isn't to dismiss her feelings by saying, "You're wrong about the time." It's to acknowledge her feelings by saying, "You're right about feeling left alone."

This response would have changed the course of their evening:

> **Her:** "You ruined our night! You've been inside fiddling with the TV for an hour!"

> **Him:** "You know something... you're right. Getting this dumb TV to work took away from our time together, didn't it? My bad."

> **To his daughters:** "Girls, you're on your own! Play a game or watch the movie on your iPad. Don't interrupt us unless the house catches on fire."

To his wife: "Let's get back in that jacuzzi and pick up where we left off. I've been waiting all week to have a little one-on-one time with my beautiful wife."

RNR = Romantic Night Resumed!

This is how you turn a point of *contention* into a point of *connection*.

Guys, you can do this! I was the poster child for weak and passive husbands. I'm a different man today.

Start with baby steps.

YOUR CLIFF NOTES[27]

These six bullet points are worth the price of the book. Commit them to memory:

- Most women process out loud. By talking. Stop wishing they didn't! When your wife vents, share the moment with her. Process with her. This is how you build closeness and intimacy.

- Women don't typically come out and say what they want. Instead, they drop a few crumbs to see if we care enough to follow the trail.

- Our winning percentages go way up when we tune in to what's *not* being said by our spouse.

- Your wife's invitation to build relational intimacy will often be *un*-inviting. It might be veiled as a complaint or an accusation.

- The hot-button issue at hand is hardly ever the real issue. That means the hero move is rarely on the surface. It's rarely obvious. It will require some digging.

- A Level-Five Husband turns a point of contention into a point of connection.

PUT IT TO WORK

1. When your wife complains or says something cryptic or crazy and you're tempted to dismiss her, ask yourself, "How can I take her side? How can I process this with her?" Your starting point can be as simple as, "You sound upset. Tell me more."

2. Grow your self-awareness muscle by tuning in to what your wife *isn't* saying. Look past what feels like an overreaction — anger or frustration over something minor — and identify the deeper issue. The one lurking beneath the surface.

3. Acknowledge the deeper issue. Talk about it. See if you can get your wife to open up.

4. What did you learn? Grab your journal and write it down. Or maybe you blew it. Good! Do what I do. Replay the episode in your mind then script what would have been a stronger response. This primes your brain to find the hero move next time.

And yes, there will be a next time.

The Hidden Source of Tension

You have a perfect system for getting the results you're getting.
−RICH LITVIN

Many of us have an unwritten, unspoken marriage contract with our spouse. The contract, of course, includes sex. In all honesty, for most men, the contract *hinges* on sex. It's a sex contract.

"I provide a service, you give me sex in return."

Mine sounded something like this:

"I work hard and earn a decent living, you give me sex."

Or, depending on the day of the week:

- "I pitch in and do a few household chores, you give me sex."

- "I don't look at other women, you give me sex."

- "I throw you a bone in the form of an occasional date night, you give me sex."

Hardly romantic.

And worlds apart from the original contract — the one we publicly agreed to on our wedding day. Here's a portion of it. You'll notice there's no mention of its pending revision:

> To have and to hold
> To love and to cherish
> For better or for worse
> Till death do us part

Most likely, you vowed something similar. And most likely, you've revised the contract once or twice since then. To be fair, it only exists on a subconscious level. You're not aware of it as you go about your day — listening to a podcast, scooping out the inside of an avocado, saying goodnight to your kids — but it's there. It colors everything in your marriage.

It also creates a plethora of problems. Here's why:

Your wife doesn't know it exists.

It's never been verbalized. It's not in writing. There was no formal gathering or ceremony to amend the original contract.

This conversation never took place:

> **You:** "Hey babe, I know this is a surprise, but I've invited our parents, siblings, and closest friends to the house this Saturday."
>
> **Her:** "Really?! This Saturday?! What for?"

You: "I want to renew our marriage vows."

[swoon]

Her: "O, honey! That is soooooo romantic."

[kiss, kiss, kiss, kiss, kiss]

"What prompted this?"

You: "Well, remember our original marriage vows — to have and to hold, to love and to cherish, yada, yada?"

Her: "Of course, my love."

You: "I've decided to amend them slightly."

Her: "Amend them?"

You: "The whole thing was kind of wordy, you know? I trimmed the first few lines. And the "for better or for worse" part feels unreasonable. I removed that, too. Actually, I got rid of everything. The new contract reads, 'I hold a job and pay the bills, you give me sex.' Simple, right? Guests will be arriving at 5:00."

BAIT AND SWITCH

Here's the other big issue with revising your marriage contract:

Your wife really, really, really likes the old one.

It's the one she's still holding you to. It's the one she's still measuring you by. And it's the path she's still hoping you'll lead her down.

This is where the tension in your home comes from.

It doesn't come from your different communication styles — she's headline, you're fine print. Or your different tastes in music — she's Tim McGraw, you're Jack White. Or your different circadian rhythms — she's early bird, you're night owl.

It comes from the dissonance created by the two contracts.

If you live in a two-contract household, your wife feels lost. Untethered. Like she's in a bad dream — where the floor beneath her has given way and she's in free fall, anticipating the splat.

Something has changed, but she can't quite put her finger on it. It's the same house, same furniture, same toothpaste, and same faces at the dinner table... but something is off.

It gnaws at her.

Now you understand why there's chronic, low-grade resentment running through your home.

- She resents you replacing the old contract with the new one.

- She resents you obligating her to terms she never agreed to.

- She resents you guilting her (and silently punishing her) for not fulfilling those terms.

- She resents you acting like *she's* the source of the problem.

- And she resents herself for not seeing this coming.

And what about you?

I'm guessing you feel frustrated.

I sure did.

Coercing my wife into bed so she could fulfill her half of the imaginary contract was always a struggle. Holding a job and paying the bills hardly ever resulted in passionate lovemaking. More often than not, sex was hollow. The kind you'd expect from a one-sided contract. And my wife grew harder and more dismissive by the day.

Laughably, when she filed for divorce, I protested, "Our marriage contract is sacred in God's eyes! How dare you break it!"

What a jackass.

God loved the old contract. He *hated* the new one.

THREE ROADS DIVERGED IN A WOOD

If any of this rings true, here are your three options:

1. **Do nothing** — It's the least disruptive of the three, primarily because it's remarkably similar to your current course of action. Simply sit back, follow the crowd, and watch the frustration in your marriage reach unbearable levels until one of you relieves the pressure by having an affair or filing for divorce.

For the record, I don't recommend "Do nothing," but it's certainly within your rights. At the very least, it allows you to fulfill the ancient proverb, "As a dog returns to its vomit, so a fool repeats his foolishness."[28] That counts for something.

2. **Ask your wife to revise _her_ vows** — Something like, "You take out the trash, I give you sex." Now, I don't know your wife, but I'm going to label this a long shot. Webster's defines long shot as "A venture unlikely to succeed; an entry (as in a horse race) given little chance of winning."[29] With that said, there's always hope. You might catch her on a good day. My only suggestion is to put it in writing and have her sign it in front of a notary public _before_ you invite family and friends to the vow renewal ceremony.

3. **Live up to the original contract** — This is the most promising of the three. The most demanding. The most rewarding. If you go back and read it, you'll find the original contract is actually your yellow brick road. The path to your higher self. Your stronger self. Your Maximus self.

Ironically, it's also the path to crazy-good sex.

Rip up the counterfeit contract.

Live up to the original one.

What one can be, one _must_ be. (Abraham Maslow)

WHAT ABOUT HER?

Some of you are asking: "Fine, I'll keep my end of the bargain, but what about her?!"

Hmmm, that's a good one. She also set the bar very high, right? To love and cherish *you*.

But here's the thing, "What about her?" isn't part of the original contract — only the conditional one.

Here's a much better question:

> What kind of man will I become if I live up to *my* half of the contract?
>
> If I choose generosity.
>
> If I throw away the scorecard.
>
> If I love her when she deserves it and when she doesn't.
>
> If I meet her needs before she meets mine.
>
> If I move toward her and not away from her (even on her "for worse" days).
>
> If I feel her pain before attempting to fix her problem.
>
> What kind of man will I become?

How about...

Strong. Valiant. Honorable. Compassionate. Gentle. Fierce.

Alive.

My advice?

Do you.

Focus on what you *can* control, not what you can't.

> Consider how hard it is to change yourself and you'll understand what little chance you have to change someone else. (Jacob Braude)

PUT IT TO WORK

1. What's your unwritten, unspoken marriage contract with your spouse? Write it down.

2. How has it hurt your marriage?

3. List the ways you've "punished" your wife for not fulfilling her half of the imaginary contract.

4. Tell her what you've learned. Then reaffirm your commitment to live up to the original contract.

5. Read your vows together. Post them prominently throughout your home. Review them daily.

6. Pick a date and plan a vow renewal ceremony. (I'll officiate it if you'd like.)

Now go breathe fire.

Your Wife and Her Dumb Ideas

A woman is to be loved, not understood.
That is the first understanding.

—OSHO

We all know what this is like:

Seemingly out of nowhere, your wife has an awesome idea! It's something she's really excited about, so she sends you a text with lots of exclamation marks and emojis.

Except *you* think it's the dumbest thing you've ever heard.

Your first response — which thankfully she can't see — is to scrunch your face, shake your head dismissively from side to side, and snap, *"What?!"*

In this chapter, I'm going to answer two very important questions:

1. What's *really* going on? (It's not what you think.)

2. How should I respond when my wife proposes something I think is foolish or impractical?

DUMB AND DUMBER

Let's look at a real-life example of a wife with a dumb idea. First, some context: I have a client in the Pacific Northwest whose wife felt invisible and alone in their marriage for over a decade. Rather than slowly asphyxiate, she put their relationship on pause, asked him to move out for 12 months, and insisted he hire me.

Smart woman.

But last week she had a *really* dumb idea. Just two months into their 12-month experiment, she sent her husband this text:

> Hey, I just saw a house for sale in that neighborhood we love. It's closer to the kids' school, has an extra bedroom and a full basement! Can we go see it? 😊😊😊

His first impulse was to write back, *"Are you insane?!"*

Fortunately, he toned it down and replied, "How is that a good idea right now?"

Understandable, given his situation. But unwise, given his situation. He missed a red-carpet opportunity to connect with his wife.

A BID FOR CONNECTION

In a moment, I'm going to give you what would have been the perfect response to his wife's "dumb" idea. But first, let's answer question number one: When your wife sends you a text like the one above, what's *really* going on?

Here's what you need to know:

It's not about the house. It's not about the neighborhood. It's not about the basement or extra bedroom. She's making what leading marriage authority John Gottman calls "a bid for connection." A bid is a question, statement, touch, or look that says, "I want to feel connected to you."

When his wife asks, "Can we go see the house?" she's not looking for information. She's not even looking for an answer — yes, no, or maybe. She's looking to connect with her husband on a deeper level than laundry, bills, and what's for dinner.

Look again at her text:

> Hey, I just saw a house for sale in that neighborhood we love. It's closer to the kids' school, has an extra bedroom and a full basement! Can we go see it? 😊😊😊

That neighborhood *we* love.

Huge.

She's taking a risk. She wants to believe her husband is for real. She wants to believe he loves her enough to evolve. She's dreaming about a future together with him and how awesome it could be!

But instead of joining her in that moment, he turned her away.

His response — "How is that a good idea right now?" — reinforced her feelings of detachment and left her thinking, "We'll *never* be on the same page."

Here's the crazy thing: We want our wives to invite us in sexually, yet we say, "Nah," when they invite us in emotionally. We're not willing to connect with them in the ways *they* prefer, but throw a fit when they won't connect with us (have sex) in the ways *we* prefer.

Now *that's* dumb.

CONNECT FIRST, ASK QUESTIONS LATER

Some of you have a natural tendency to be business-like. It's a strength. You don't waste time. You get things done!

But unless self-awareness is also a strength, there are times when being business-like will sour the moment. Push others away. Cost us an opportunity to connect and bond with the people we love.

Relationships are all about connection.

That evening I said to my client, "From now on, forget the details. Don't try to dot every i and cross every t. Don't even try to figure out whether your wife's idea is a really good one or a really bad one. Leave that for later. Just be present. *Connect* with her."

Here's the mantra I wrote for him:

> The point is connection. I can ask questions later. I can voice objections later. I can come up with a plan and put all the ducks in a row later. My first priority is to connect with my wife and children.

The abridged version is a little easier to remember and has been serving him well:

> Connect first, ask questions later.

HOW TO RESPOND

OK, let's get really practical. What would have been a much better response (which he sent the next day) to his wife's "dumb" idea?

Here's the first line:

> You're right, we *do* love that neighborhood.

Feel the difference?!

Everything about that one line says *connection*. It says, "Us!" It says, "You and me, baby!" If your last name is Collins, it screams, "TEAM COLLINS!" in capital letters.

Here's where it gets really good:

> You're right, we *do* love that neighborhood. What's the address? I'm going to email the listing agent and set up a time for us to see it. Saturday morning is good for you, right?

BOOM.

Connect first, ask questions later.

PUSHBACK

I can hear some of you protesting, "But Jeff, what if I was in this husband's shoes and already know we can't afford it?!"

I get it... neither can they.

But right now it doesn't matter.

Connecting with her is what matters. Enjoying a shared moment with her is what matters. Walking through a beautiful home together and dreaming of what's possible is what matters.

I'm not saying to write an offer on the home!

Maybe her idea *is* impractical. But moments like these — when she feels cherished — give birth to greater moments of healing and intimacy.

Imagine you were this husband.

Imagine your wife smiling and bouncing through her dream home that Saturday morning. The tour ends and the real estate agent says, "I'm going to step outside and give you two a little privacy, so you can talk things over."

That's your cue to grab her hand, look her in the eyes and say, "I'd love to see us in a home like this. The kitchen has everything you've ever wanted. And that extra bedroom could be your office."

She chimes in, "And the kids could walk to school! What do think, honey? Are we anywhere close to affording a home like this?"

"I don't know. Let's sit down and crunch the numbers. But here's what I do know: I would give *anything* to have more moments like this with you. It crushes me to know I've been the kind of husband who made his wife feel invisible for so long. I can't imagine what I've put you through. I'm so sorry, honey. I took so much for granted. Would you forgive me?"

A moment like that can heal a thousand hurts.

Remember...

Your wife's dumb ideas are only *disguised* as dumb ideas. They're actually red-carpet opportunities to build closeness and connection and intimacy.

Connect, when?

First.

Connect first, ask questions later.

Go Big

*The world of the generous gets larger and larger. The world
of the stingy gets smaller and smaller.*[30]

—PROVERBS 11:24

Generosity is counterintuitive.

It means loving your wife when she least deserves it. It means
giving more than is required. It means taking off your score-
keeping glasses.

In relationships, it's the opposite of Janet Jackson's refrain, "What
have you done for me lately?"[31]

Is God (or the universe) nudging you toward being more generous
in your marriage? If so, know this: He's about to *enlarge* you, not
diminish you. Make you *more* powerful, not less.

Generosity changes people. It softens hearts. Unsticks the stuck.
Ends arguments. Grows strong and sexy marriages.

You can play small or you can change the world by being generous,
but you can't do both.

AN EXPERIMENT

Intimate relationships provide us with multiple opportunities (daily) to choose between stinginess and generosity.

What if you turned every potential annoyance in your marriage into a growth moment? An opportunity to stretch yourself and become a larger and more likable you. An opportunity to be a little more generous...

A little more patient.

A little more helpful.

A little more lenient.

A little more tuned in to what's *not* being said.

A little warmer.

A little kinder.

A little faster to forgive.

A little swifter to issue a pardon.

A little quicker to believe the best.

A little slower to criticize.

A little slower to take it personally.

A little slower to erect walls.

You might be surprised at what happens.

Your marriage just might break out of its box and morph into the close and intimate one you've both been aching for.

> There's no such thing as a small act of kindness. Every act creates a ripple with no logical end. (Scott Adams)

Kick stingy to the curb this week.

Be a wife magnet.

PUT IT TO WORK

1. Ask, "Where am I cutting corners? Where am I giving a little but expecting a lot?"

2. Ask, "What don't I like about our marriage right now? In light of this chapter, what opportunity does that present me with?"

3. Are you waiting to *get* more before you *give* more? As you wait, what are you withholding from your wife? Is it warmth, affection, compliments, hugs, quality time? Does this feel strong or weak to you?

4. Reverse course. Pick one thing you could do *this week* to stretch yourself, be more generous, and love your wife when she least deserves it.

5. Do it! Then text or call me and tell me how strong that feels. My cell phone number is (818) 209-6294. (Yes, that's my real number.)

The Oxymoron That Could Heal (and Even Save) Your Marriage

We were together. I forget the rest.
–WALT WHITMAN

Webster's defines oxymoron as "A combination of contradictory or incongruous words."[32] Here are a few of my favorite:

Freezer burn, pretty ugly, loose tights, soft rock, numb feeling, minor crisis, only choice, growing smaller, random order, jumbo shrimp, and — quite possibly the most wickedly ingenious phrase ever devised by evil marketers and foisted upon unsuspecting consumers like us — shop 'n save.

I doubt you're aware of it, but your wife has a favorite oxymoron. It's even more intriguing to her subconscious mind than the aforementioned shop 'n save. I talk to married women across the country and it's abundantly clear. The oxymoron that revs their engine most is this one:

Alone together.

It's also what your marriage needs more of.

Time.

Just the two of you.

No kids. No distractions. No laptops. No dishes in the sink. Just the two of you.

Alone. Together.

A TALE OF TWO TRIPS

A friend and his wife vacationed in Europe last summer. Three whole weeks. Just the two of them. I saw him recently and asked, "How was your trip?" His answer is what prompted this chapter. His answer is what got me thinking about oxymorons and missed opportunities.

He said, "I didn't realize it, but it's what our marriage desperately needed. English isn't spoken in the villages we visited, so we literally had no one else to talk to. It was like God set us up! We talked about everything. We shared everything. There was more touching, more laughing, more lovemaking, more handholding, more affection ... it's the closest we've been in years. We're still enjoying the afterglow of those three weeks together."

A few days later, I bumped into another friend. He's an admitted workaholic whose insignificant other had just informed him she's moving to a different city in six months (without him). He's taking the there's-nothing-i-can-do-about-it-so-i'll-just-wait-

and-see approach. I get it, he feels defeated, but I told him to order *Wife Magnet* immediately. He'll quickly realize "I'm moving to a different city in six months," is her way of saying, "*I'm dying!* I feel alone in our marriage! I can't do this for much longer!"

I also told him to drag "wait-and-see" into the backyard and fire a few slugs through its thick skull.

That brings us to you.

You may not have the luxury of enjoying a 3-week European vacation, but you do have an hour to take your shoes off, hold her hand, and walk on the beach this weekend. You do have $50 for a few drinks at the local watering hole. You might even have $500 for a few nights out of town. With a little initiative and effort, there's *something* you can do to feed your marriage. Have you held it up to a mirror lately? It's probably looking a little lean. And like my first friend discovered, just-the-two-of-you time could be what it's starving for.

Here's what alone-together time says to your spouse:

- "You still do it for me."
- "There's no one I'd rather be with."
- "I love being married to you."
- "Nothing is more important to me than *us*."

So, when you pitch your wife with a walk on the beach, or drinks this Friday night, or a brief jaunt out of town, remember to use her favorite oxymoron:

"Wouldn't that be fun? Just the two of us. Alone together."

BAM.

PUT IT TO WORK

1. One of the most toxic and destructive lies I believed as a husband was self-perpetuating and sounded something like this: "Yeah, work is a little crazy right now, but things will slow down soon and then we'll spend more time together, I promise! Just gotta get through this month (or this quarter)."

   That was mine. What's yours?

2. What's one alone-together activity you can put on the calendar right now?

3. Do it.

4. Big picture, what needs to change? About your life? Your schedule? Your priorities?

5. Act now. Today you have options, tomorrow you may not.

Urgent things shout, important things whisper. Listen to the whispers. (Ken Groen)

An Attribute of the Strong

Reject your sense of injury and the injury itself disappears.
—MARCUS AURELIUS

I officiated a wedding last Saturday. The bride and groom asked me to read a short passage from the New Testament that contains this line: "Love keeps no record of being wronged."[33]

Poetic, isn't it?

So poetic, in fact, it's easy to miss the impact of that statement.

Keeps no record ... of being wronged.

Wronged!

Someone did you wrong.

Don't minimize it. Don't skirt around it. Don't lie to yourself and say, "Well, it was no big deal." *No! Someone did you wrong.* A real crime was committed. Maybe it was a misdemeanor. Maybe it was a full-blown felony. But trust was breached. Someone *hurt* you.

I help husbands get unstuck and bring sexy back, so let's put this in marriage terms:

Your wife hurt you.

Your wife — your babydoll, your sweetheart, your best girl, your main squeeze, your partner, your va-va-voom, your better half, your beautiful bride — did you wrong. She did something hurtful.

- She rolled her eyes at you.

- She jerked her hand away as you reached for it.

- She verbally assaulted you in front of her parents.

- She snapped at you in front of the kids.

- She got up and walked out of the room when you walked in.

Or maybe it came in the form of words:

- "I can't believe I married you."

- "My last boyfriend never would've done that."

- "You act more like a woman than a man in this relationship."

- "I wish you were more like your brother."

- "Come home from work whenever you want. Whatever. I don't care."

Ouch.

Remember the wedding I mentioned? Here's a brief excerpt from my sermonette that day:

—————————

From the Sermon on the Mount...

> When someone gives you a hard time, respond with the energy of prayer and good deeds. This is what God does. He gives his best — the sun to warm and the rain to nourish — to everyone, regardless: the good and bad, the nice and nasty. If all you do is love the lovable, do you expect a bonus? Anybody can do that. If you simply say hello to those who greet you, do you expect a medal? Any run-of-the-mill sinner does that. In a word, what I'm saying is, grow up. Live generously and graciously toward others, the way God lives toward you.[34]

What is Jesus saying here to married couples?

He's saying, "Anyone can love their spouse when it's easy! *Big freaking deal.* The real question is: Do you love your husband when he's insensitive and uncaring? Do you love your wife when she overreacts and withdraws physically and emotionally?"

King Solomon wrote:

> It's the glory of a man to overlook an offense.[35]

"Glory" isn't a word we use very often. Here's the contextual meaning — "This is our highest attribute on display."

In other words:

We're at our *best* when we overlook an offense.

We're at our *best* when we forgive the person who wronged us.

We're at our *best* when we refuse to keep score.

Gandhi said it this way:

> The weak can never forgive. Forgiveness is an attribute
> of the strong.

Settle this in your mind once and for all ...

Forgiveness isn't weak!

Loving people when they least deserve it isn't weak!

It's mighty.

It's powerful.

It's acting like God.

This might be where some of you are stuck.

I write about being a warrior. Getting off the hamster wheel and fighting for your wife's heart. Loving her and pursuing her even when she acts unlovely. But let's face it, you're not going anywhere near her if you're holding onto an offense.

You're right, what she said was hurtful. You're right, she should know better. You're right, she doesn't deserve to be let off the hook this time.

But isn't that the point? None of us *deserve* forgiveness. Forgiveness is a gift. It's a gift we choose to give someone. A gift they could never earn. You certainly don't owe it to her, but you do owe it to yourself and to your marriage.

Remember the "for better or for worse" part of your marriage vows? Yeah, well, your wife acting unlovable is one of those "for worse" moments. But guess what? "Better" always follows close on the heels of "worse." Forgiving your spouse when she least deserves it makes *you* a better man. A better person. It makes you stronger. More powerful. More generous. More gracious.

And if we believe what the rabbi said, more like God.

1. ACKNOWLEDGE THE OFFENSE

First, call it what it is:

> "My wife snapped at me in front of the kids. Her words were hurtful and embarrassing. I can still remember the looks on their faces. I'm pissed off because we agreed to never argue in front of them!"

Don't push the pain away. *Feel it.* Grieve it if you need to.

2. CHOOSE TO FORGIVE

Second, choose to forgive her for it.

Take a moment. Say it out loud:

> "I don't feel like forgiving her. I feel like hurting her. Like treating her the way she treated me. But I choose forgiveness instead. I choose strength and generosity instead. Maybe she's hurting inside. Maybe she's angry at herself and took it out on me. I don't know, but I choose to believe she's a better woman than this.

> "[Your wife's name], I forgive you. I tear up the record of how you wronged me. In this family, we refuse to keep score. We forgive each other. We believe the best about each other. We love each other, not just when it's easy — any pansy can do that — but when it's hard, and I'm setting the example right now! I'm changing the atmosphere in our home right now! I'm crushing the head of the serpent right now!"

This is what men do.

This is what it sounds like to be the head of your home.

[**Note:** Choosing forgiveness might include an honest talk with your spouse about her behavior. Do that! Speak up for yourself. But do it in the spirit I've presented here. Not to hurt her back, but to restore your connection. To strengthen your marriage. Make it a growth moment for both of you.]

LEAD THE CHARGE

One morning, my wife said something ugly and hurtful as I was getting ready to walk out the door and head to the office. As soon as I pulled out of our driveway, I did two things: Right there, in the privacy of my Jetta, I acknowledged what she did and how it made me feel, then I opened my mouth and released a torrent of forgiveness in her direction. I chose the strength Gandhi spoke of. The generosity Jesus spoke of.

Five minutes later, my cell phone rang. It was her. Not the "her" I had left at home, but an altogether different "her." The softer and more tender version. The one who loved and adored her husband.

> **Me:** "Hey, babe."
>
> **Her:** "Hi, honey ... um ... can I get a do-over? I was a bit of a jerk this morning. It's no excuse, but I have a presentation at 11:00, and I'm feeling a little under-prepared, and ... well, the stress got to me. I didn't mean what I said. Not even close. I called to say I'm sorry. Would you forgive me?"
>
> (Little did she know, I already had.)
>
> **Me:** "Of course, baby. Damn, I totally forgot about your presentation. Would you forgive *me* for not being more in tune with you and what you needed this morning? I want to be a better husband than that. You're my Number One."

BOOM.

What could have taken days or weeks to sort through was over in a matter of minutes. We were acting like a couple of lovebirds before I reached the Hollywood Freeway.

THE LAST WORD

Oh, and I can't leave this part out. There's one more compelling reason to forgive your spouse when she least deserves it. The same guy who wrote, "Love keeps no record of being wronged," also wrote this:

> Live creatively, friends. If someone falls into sin, forgivingly restore him, saving your critical comments for yourself. You might be needing forgiveness before the day's out.[36]

And, I might add, *your* ugly moment might be a whole lot uglier than her ugly moment.

PUT IT TO WORK

1. Identify something your wife has done (or hasn't done) that's gotten under your skin. Maybe it's been bugging you for years. Maybe you've held it over her head one or two or twenty times. Don't sugar-coat it. Call it what it is. Feel the pain and injustice of that moment.

2. Use my script above and tear up the IOU you wrote. Choose generosity instead! Choose forgiveness instead! Offer it as a gift. A gift she could never earn.

Wear Out Your Mattress Springs with More of These

You are what you do, not what you say you'll do.

−CARL JUNG

In my marriage, I volunteered to do lots of things that I never did. Not in a timely fashion, at least.

Her: "We need to make an appointment with our tax guy."

Me: "I'll call him this week."

Her: "One of our sprinkler heads is broken, and the grass in our front yard is turning brown."

Me: "No problem. I'll replace it this weekend."

Her: "Can you help me upload the photos on my camera? It's such a pain."

Me: "Sure. Just leave it on my dresser and I'll take care of it for you."

If you've been married more than a month, you know what's coming next.

The question.

Oh, it might not come for a week or two, but it's coming.

- "Did you call our tax guy?"
- "Did you fix the sprinkler?"
- "Can I have my camera back?"

Far too often, instead of owning it like a man, I stuttered and stammered my way into deeper doo-doo.

> **Me:** "Uh, let me think … tax guy … did I make that call? Hmmm. I remember I was going to. Oh wait, that's right, I was about to call him and set up our appointment when I got pulled into a meeting. Crap! I'll do it this week."
>
> **Her:** "*This week?! Aauuugghh!* It should have been done months ago! Why didn't you call him *last* week like you said you would?!"
>
> **Me:** "I didn't have time."

[sound of my parachute not opening]

Here's what "I didn't have time" really means and what every frustrated woman hears in that moment:

"I really don't care that you lose sleep at night worrying about our taxes. I really don't care that our front yard is ugly and embarrasses you. I really don't care that you're stressed out and fearful we might lose our family photos from summer vacation. What matters to you doesn't matter to me. *You* don't matter to me. I have lots of priorities, but you're not one of them. There are important people in my life, but you're not one of them. You're practically last in line."

Fool.

I actively eroded the foundations of security, trust, respect, and intimacy in my marriage and wasn't even aware of it.

EXECUTION IS KING

> You can't build a reputation on what you're *going* to do.
> (Henry Ford)

I unfairly wanted my wife to judge me — not by what I did — but by what I *intended* to do. By what I was *going* to do. I never afforded her the same luxury, of course, but held her to a much higher standard, judging and evaluating her strictly by her actions.

Jung was right: We are what we do, not what we say we'll do. Pledges, promises, vows, verbal commitments, words, deadlines, and other people's praises don't shape our wife's perception of us. Only our actions do. Only our follow-throughs do.

In the world of women, execution is king.

Good intentions weigh less than a dryer sheet.

MASTER THE ART OF ONE-SIDED CONVERSATIONS

When you volunteer to do something, write it down. Schedule it. Prioritize it.

Prioritize *her*.

That's always what this is about.

Better yet, anticipate her needs and take charge! From Chapter 5 of *Wife Magnet*: "Intimate and lasting marriages are forged when we anticipate the day-to-day needs of our wives, tap into our masculine energy stores, and spring into action *before* we're asked."

> **You:** "I saw tax forms on your desk the other day, and I know how much you hate it when we fall behind. I called our accountant this morning. Our appointment is next Tuesday at 4:00 PM. Is there anything else we need for that meeting? Bank statements? W-2's?"

> **You:** "Hey babe, I keep meaning to fix that broken sprinkler head, but weekends have been so busy since Little League started. It's my only time with the boys. The good news is I found a handyman who can do it this Saturday for only $50. I know you're tired of our front yard looking so ugly."

> **You:** "You were having trouble with your camera, right? I went ahead and created a new Dropbox folder named *Summer Vacation 2022* and uploaded all those awesome pictures you took. I also changed the settings on your camera, so whenever you connect it to your laptop, new photos will upload automatically to the

cloud. You don't have to worry about losing them ever again! I tested it and it works great. I can show you right now if you have a minute." (I'm guessing, but you might need more than a minute. Especially if her laptop is in the bedroom.)

Trust me... you'll learn to *love* these one-sided conversations.

PUT IT TO WORK

The things that get scheduled are the things that get done. Until you schedule something, it's only a concept, and extraordinary people don't build extraordinary lives on concepts. They build their lives on action and execution. *They get things done.* (Robin Sharma)

OK, now it's your turn.

1. What's one thing your wife needs you to take care of? She's brought it up more than once. You've written it and re-written it on multiple to-do lists.

2. When will you *do* what you volunteered to do?

3. Excellent! Plan and schedule it now. (Yes, now.)

4. Follow through. *Do it.* Build a reputation for being a husband who gets things done!

Bringing Sexy Back

Zach took his jacket off and draped it around my shoulders,
which (according to Liz, who double-checked with Macy)
is the single sexiest thing a guy can do.[37]

−ALLY CARTER

Being kind is sexy.

Being thoughtful is sexy.

Giving her a 5-minute shoulder massage is sexy.

Turning off SportsCenter and going to bed when she does is sexy.

Holding her when she's sad is sexy.

Saving the last container of organic, whole milk, honey vanilla greek yogurt for her is sexy.

6-pack abs don't hurt, of course, but a flat stomach will never trump kindness or empathy.

Now you know.

No Comprendo

Love until it feels like love to the other person.
—MARIANNE WILLIAMSON

According to Dr. Gary Chapman, there are five love languages:[38]

1. Words of Affirmation

2. Gifts

3. Acts of Service

4. Quality Time

5. Physical Touch

My son's love language is Quality Time. Giving him my undivided attention.

Growing up, it was always, "Daddy, come play," "Daddy, come sit," "Daddy, come watch."

Gifts, no matter how thoughtful, don't feel like love to him. Acts of Service, no matter how selfless, don't feel like love to him. Just-the-two-of-us-time is what feels like love to him.

You can see the problem this presents in marriage.

What if, like my son, your wife's primary love language is Quality Time, but yours is Acts of Service?

> **You:** "Hey babe, I noticed the red 'change oil' light was on in your car. I ran it over to Jiffy Lube this morning and took care of it for you."
>
> **Her:** "OK. Have you seen my keys?"
>
> **You:** "The lavender you planted out front looks great! How 'bout I weed those flower beds for you tomorrow?"
>
> **Her:** "Whatever floats your boat."

And while you're thinking, "Tonight's gonna be a good, good night," it's the furthest thing from *her* mind, because her Quality Time love tank is bone dry.

For her, taking a walk together feels like love. Going to bed when she does feels like love. Turning your phone off during a conversation feels like love.

And there you are — superhero husband — pulling weeds and swatting horse flies on a sweltering August afternoon to no avail.

Thoughtful, well-intentioned, but sex-starved.

You could've hired a gardner, taken your wife out for drinks, and had a *much* better night.

DECISION TIME

Moving forward, you have two miles-apart options:

1. Beat your head against the same wall. (You'll need one of these — amzn.to/35ngYnE)

2. Learn to speak her love language. (Read *The 5 Love Languages* by Gary Chapman.)

My suggestion?

Grow.

Stretch yourself.

Learn to speak her love language.

> You'll be glad every night that you treated her right.[39]
> (George Thorogood)

Choose Your Pain

There are two pains in life: the pain of discipline or the pain of regret. One weighs ounces, the other weighs tons.

–JIM ROHN

Here's something you didn't know:

A "sexless marriage" isn't a marriage without sex.

Dr. Rachel Becker-Warner, a relationship and sex therapist from the Program in Human Sexuality at the University of Minnesota, defines it as "any partnership where sexual intimacy occurs 10 times or less within a one-year period."[40]

Some of you are doing the math in your head right now. Others are thinking, "I *wish* it was 10 times a year. More like 3-4."

I've been there.

And rather than face the pain of a marriage that was unraveling and do the hard work of fixing what was broken, I stuffed my feelings and stayed on the hamster wheel.

Looking back, I wish like hell someone had told me what I'm about to tell you:

Your marriage is begging for a hero.

It's true.

There's a knight in shining armor in your wife's future. It might be you (she secretly hopes so), it might be someone else (let's call him Rebound Guy), but that vacancy *will* be filled.

Your wife can temporarily shelve physical intimacy, but her need for closeness and emotional intimacy never goes away.

OPPORTUNITY KNOCKS

Let's face it, if you keep your head in the sand, Rebound Guy will have it easy. The early stages of romantic attraction are intense and intoxicating. Teeming with sexual tension. Oxytocin and dopamine are flying off the shelves.

But if you fetch your armor from the attic and choose the hero's path, *hard* will be your constant companion. There will be obstacles to overcome. Issues to work through. Old wounds to heal. Character flaws to fix.

And therein lies the opportunity...

The next level of your marriage demands a different you.

It means you get to grow and evolve and become the hero your family is crossing its fingers for — a bigger, bolder, more present, powerful, loving, kind, tenacious, eye-of-the-tiger YOU.

All Rebound Guy has to do is remain a putz.

Which brings us to your two opposing choices:

1. Go big and do the hard work of fixing what's broken in your marriage.

2. Play small and let your marriage run its likely course.

[sarcasm alert]

The second option is *much* easier. Plus, there's a huge upside.

You get to hook up with someone else!

Most likely a woman who's unhappy in her marriage or a divorcée on the rebound, in which case *you* get to be the putz who refused to grow. Who was afraid to face his inadequacies as a husband. You and all of your blind spots, old wounds, and personal character flaws get to waltz right into your next relationship.

Now you understand why 67% of all second marriages end in divorce.

THE HERO'S PATH

Option one is the road less traveled and the one I help men navigate. The hero's path is treacherous. Bloody. It's fraught with dragons, wars, moats, and miscreants. You'll notice the glaring lack of creature comforts and half-assed enterprises. And there's no whining on the hero's path. No pouting. No excuse-making.

Best of all?

No regrets.

You won't find a single one.

What you *will* find is courage, honor, and men worth following.

#TTFUBC

I had a new client who kept saying things like, "I did what you said yesterday, and dude, it's working!" Or, "Remember that card you helped me write? I left it on her pillow this morning and *boom!* I have my wife back!"

Then a day or two later he'd be ready to call it quits, because she refused him sex or didn't respond to something the way he had hoped.

My brothers, in life there is good pain … and there is bad pain.

The greatest pain I've ever felt wasn't the day my wife moved out. It wasn't the Christmas morning she came to the door with presents for our son — dressed to the nines — on her way to see someone else. It wasn't even the moment I stood before a judge and silently wept as he pronounced the end of our marriage.

No, the greatest pain I've ever felt is with me right now. It's the pain of realizing the woman I married will never know this me. She'll never know New Jeff. She'll never experience or enjoy the man I am today. *Ever.*

That's good pain.

The pain of growth and change and no regrets.

Embrace it.

Then there's the pain of staying a schmuck. The pain of shortcuts and pity parties and unbridled anger posing as masculinity.

That's bad pain.

Run from it.

PUT IT TO WORK

1. **Build your awareness muscle** — Notice moments throughout the day when you bump into pain or discomfort and ask yourself, "In light of the marriage I want, is this the kind of pain I should avoid or move toward?" If it's a hot stove, avoid it. Everything else, move toward it!

2. **Do things that suck** — In order to evolve, have our wives swoon over us, and become men worth following, we need to fundamentally change our relationship with pain. My aversion to pain and addiction to comfort were the reasons I squandered my marriage. It's why I begin each day lying on a

prickly acupressure mat, swigging shots of apple cider vinegar, running wind sprints, and immersing myself in ice cold water. They're all really good for me and they all suck! Moving *toward* discomfort every morning flips a switch in my brain that says, "I'm not looking for an easy way out today. I know that the success I want — in business, health, and relationships — is on the other side of pain. The other side of hard. The other side of suck. Bring it on, baby! I eat pain and discomfort for breakfast!"

3. **Run toward your Goliath** — What uncomfortable but good-for-you activity have you been avoiding? Maybe it's rebooting an exercise regimen. Maybe it's getting up a little earlier to read or meditate. Maybe it's having a hard talk with someone you love. Or forgiving someone from your past. Maybe it's calling a marriage counselor. Listen to your inner wisdom and run *toward* the thing you've been avoiding. You're a stronger and better man on the other side of this battle.

4. **Become the hero your wife is crossing her fingers for** — I'll talk more about that in the next (and final) chapter.

How to Stay in Beast Mode

Falling in love requires a pulse. Staying in love requires a plan.
−ANDY STANLEY

You've reached the last chapter, but your journey doesn't end here. Remember what I said many pages ago. You're holding this book because something nudged you toward it. Something whispered:

"Playing small is no longer an option. Staying on the hamster wheel is no longer an option. Tolerating a tepid marriage is no longer an option. There's untapped greatness inside you."

Now — 31 chapters later — your masculine heart has awoken. Your inner hero has awoken. You feel more alive than you've ever felt. And you're absolutely certain of one thing:

There's no. going. back.

This is for *life*.

In "Eyes Wide Shut," we underscored our need to be more vigilant at home. In the spirit of that chapter, let's address the greatest threat to your marriage in the weeks to come.

EVERY MAN'S BATTLE

Most men have a marriage that can only be described as "eh." So-so. Not *boo-yah*, not train wreck, just "eh."

Stuck in the mediocre middle.

Here's the head-scratcher: Like you, these men aren't jerks. Most of them are really good guys. *Then why?!* Why has the fire gone out? Why are some — unbeknownst to them — even headed for divorce?

The answer is simple.

For most husbands — even the good ones — their marriages live in the *back* of their brains. Behind work and paying bills and trying to eat right and squeezing in a workout. Waaaaay back there. That was my story. I wasn't a terrible person, but my mind wasn't on my marriage. It was on other things.

It's probably your story, too.

Today, your relationship with your wife is in the front of your brain where it belongs. And it's no accident — books like mine will do that. But over the ensuing weeks, your marriage, like a glacier, will slowly retreat to the back of your skull and settle into its former home. Sadly — *tragically* — most of the ground you've gained will be lost.

But what if...

What if there was a way to *keep* your marriage front and center? *Keep* you sharp. *Keep* you in beast mode.

Now there is.

Wife Magnet is more than a brand. It's a brotherhood. A growing alliance with one goal: to become better men. *Great* men. For ourselves, for our families, for the world.

So if playing small is no longer an option, if staying on the hamster wheel is no longer an option, if tolerating a tepid marriage is no longer an option...

Join us!

We meet online, over Zoom, and in person.

Through videos, podcasts, live Q&A events, and workshops — my team and I will help you keep your mind on your marriage. Help you keep it front and center. Help you become the hero your wife is crossing her fingers for.

It's a no-brainer :)

Drop me a line and you're in!

- jeff@wifemagnet.me

- Or visit **wifemagnet.me** to read my newest content and join our community

FOR THOSE IN CRISIS (MASTER CLASS)

When my wife began her slow exit from our marriage, I did everything wrong. I didn't know it at the time, of course, but I only pushed her further and further away. It was depressing. It was infuriating. I desperately wanted to save my marriage but didn't know *how*.

Is that you?

Is your wife checked out? Has she hinted at divorce? Maybe she's already met with a lawyer. Most likely, you're making the same mistakes I made, and things are getting worse, not better, as you had hoped. It shouldn't be surprising. None of us were taught how to do this. None of us *know* how to do this.

Not on our own.

It's why I created my Master Class and online community — so you could access the same content I walk my executive clients through. So you could enjoy the same advantages they enjoy.

I'm not a marriage coach. There are plenty of those. I'm a help-our-marriage-is-imploding-and-she's-talking-to-a-lawyer coach. I'm the guy CEO's and Grammy Award winners call when they're determined to avoid the devastation, emotional trauma, and financial bloodletting known as divorce.

My Master Class has everything you need to reverse course. To undo the damage that's been done. To move from zero to hero. Short of hiring me, it gives you the best possible chance of saving your marriage!

The Buddha said, "You *think* you have time." If your wife has one foot out the door, now is not the time to coast. Now is not the time to be conservative. Now is the time to go for broke! To push all your chips to the center of the table. To do something drastic. Remember, today you have options. Tomorrow you may not.

Access my Master Class here → **wifemagnet.me/masterclass**

> Your present circumstances don't determine where you can go; they merely determine where you start. (Nido Quebein)

CONNECT WITH ME

It's a privilege to meet one of my readers! Do you have a question, comment, or just want to say hi? I'd love to hear from you.

- (818) 209-6294
- jeff@wifemagnet.me
- Facebook / Instagram

BEFORE YOU GO...

Would you do me a favor?

If you enjoyed this book or found it helpful, would you leave a brief review on its Amazon page? Short and simple is fine. Help me bring hope and healing to more families.

Thank you!

I was a mediocre husband for 15 years. I was a superstar at work, but Rip Van Winkle at home, sleeping through most of my married life. Today, I teach husbands how to avoid the mistakes I made. How to build strong and sexy marriages. How to grow and become great men. (It's kind of an obsession.)

I'm the author of two books, host of *Wife Magnet Radio,* a marriage crisis coach, and monthly contributor at Live Free.

My real passion is my work with International Justice Mission. IJM is a human rights organization that rescues the vulnerable from sex trafficking, violence, slavery, and the abuse of power (learn more at ijm.org). Every man needs a battle to fight. This is mine.

Lastly, I'm a full-time dad, outdoor enthusiast, biohacker, soon-to-be sexagenarian, and raving fan of all things kombucha. When I'm not oversharing on Facebook, you can find me in the mountains, the ocean, or Whole Foods.

To My Scapegoat

What kind of king leaves his throne to live among addicts and crooks? To eat with outcasts. To stand up for the town slut. To quench her *real* thirst. Only you. Compassionate, fierce, faithful, and true. You walked in our shoes. You shared our sorrows. You were ravaged on that tree by our willfulness and guile.

Return, O King. We are long broken.

Endnotes

1. *Star Wars: Episode V – The Empire Strikes Back*. Screenplay by Leigh Brackett and Lawrence Kasdan. Story by George Lucas. Directed by Irvin Kershner. (20th Century Fox, 1980).

2. "Moving from Theory to Practice to Mastery" was introduced to me by my mentor and coach, Brian Johnson. https://www.heroic.us.

3. Damian Duplechain. "Relationship Tips: The Silent Male." *The Center for Marriage & Family Relationships* (March 7, 2018).

4. Sue Johnson. *Hold Me Tight* (Hatchet Book Group, 2008): 30.

5. Intimacy anorexia is a term coined by psychologist Dr. Douglas Weiss: "Intimacy anorexia is the active withholding of emotional, spiritual, and/or sexual intimacy from a spouse or significant other."

6. Dachner Keltner. "Hands On Research: The Science of Touch." *Greater Good Magazine* (September 29, 2010). The Greater Good Science Center at the University of California, Berkeley.

7. Ibid.

8. Ibid.

9. Lisa Marshall. "A Lover's Touch Eases Pain as Heartbeats, Breathing Sync." *CU Boulder Today* (June 21, 2017).

10. Ibid.

11. Ibid.

12. John Lennon and Paul McCartney. "I Want to Hold Your Hand." (Parlophone, 1963).

13. Tom Burns. "Don't be Fooled, Real Romance is All About the Little Things." *HuffPost* (September 29, 2016).

14. Ally Carter. *Once Upon a Road Trip* (Artifice Press, 2013).

15. Tony Robbins. *Live at The National Achievers Congress* (2015). Success Resources Australia.

16. Ibid.

17. Kelsea Ballerini Josh Kerr, Forest Glen Whitehead, and Lance Carpenter. "Love Me Like You Mean It." *The First Time* (Black River Entertainment, 2015).

18. Meg Selig. "Can the Novelty Habit Boost a Couple's Commitment?" *Psychology Today* (May 24, 2010)

19. Paul Byerly. "Why Wives Say No to Sex, and What a Man Can Do About It." *The Generous Husband* (June 23, 2012).

20. John Eldredge. *Wild at Heart* (Thomas Nelson, 2021).

21. James Clear. *Atomic Habits* (Penguin Random House, 2018): 34.

22. John Gottman and Nan Silver. *The Seven Principles for Making Marriage Work* (Harmony Books, 2015).

23. Ibid.

24. Gary John Bishop. *Unfu*k Yourself* (Harper Collins, 2016).

25. Marie Forleo. *Everything is Figureoutable* (Portfolio, 2020): 96.

26. I included this entire chapter from *Wife Magnet*. I consider it one of the most important things I've ever written. Porn doesn't make us weak — life does that — but it *keeps* us weak.

27. Yes, "Cliffs Notes" is the official name, but I pulled my artistic license card and chose the more commonly-used "Cliff Notes."

28. Proverbs 26:11. Taken from the Holy Bible, New Living Translation (Copyright ©1996, 2004, 2015). Used by permission of Tyndale House Publishers. All rights reserved.

29. "long shot." Merriam-Webster.com. 2022. https://www.merriam-webster.com (March 22, 2022).

30. Proverbs 11:24. Taken from THE MESSAGE (Copyright © 1993, 1994, 1995, 1996, 2000, 2001, 2002). Used by permission of NavPress Publishing Group.

31. Janet Jackson, James Harris III, and Terry Lewis. "What Have You Done for Me Lately." *Control* (A&M, 1986).

32. "oxymoron." Merriam-Webster.com. 2022. https://www.merriam-webster.com (March 22, 2022).

33. 1 Corinthians 13:5b. Taken from the Holy Bible, New Living Translation (Copyright ©1996, 2004, 2015). Used by permission of Tyndale House Publishers. All rights reserved.

34. Matthew 5:44-48. Taken from THE MESSAGE (Copyright © 1993, 1994, 1995, 1996, 2000, 2001, 2002). Used by permision of NavPress Publishing Group.

35. Proverbs 19:11b. Holy Bible, New International Version, NIV (Copyright ©1973, 1978, 1984, 2011 by Biblica, Inc.) Used by permission. All rights reserved worldwide.

36. Galatians 6:1. Taken from THE MESSAGE (Copyright © 1993, 1994, 1995, 1996, 2000, 2001, 2002). Used by permision of NavPress Publishing Group.

37. Ally Carter. *Don't Judge a Girl by Her Cover* (Disney • Hyperion Books, 2009).

38. Gary Chapman. *The 5 Love Languages* (Northfield Publishing, 2015).

39. Roy Head and Gene Kurtz. "Treat Her Right." Born to Be Bad (EMI Records, 1988).

40. Janet Brito. "Why You're Having Less Sex with Your Partner — and How to Get Back Into It." *Healthline* (January 13, 2020).

Throw away your books. Waste no more time talking about what a good man is like. Be one. (Marcus Aurelius)

Made in the USA
Columbia, SC
18 August 2023

21819584R00105